MW00607291

His Grace on a Rollercoaster

Memoirs of Dr. Mark L Jaggers

A grateful survivor

Copyright © Dr. Mark L. Jaggers 2012

Some names have been changed to protect the privacy of the individuals.

Acknowledgements

This book is dedicated to my amazing wife, Becky,
And our beautiful children, Meredith and Colin.
Together we managed to do impossible things.
Without you, I would have withered away in the storm.
Your energy and love sustained me.
Never stop loving and dreaming!
To my family, friends and the army of humanity
that carried us,
I can never repay you,
But I hope our story inspires others
to reach out to their fellow man.

To my God,
I'll never be worthy of your endless Grace,
But I will keep trying!

Foreword

This book describes the life of a remarkable man. I know many books make that claim. But what makes this one very different for me, I know this man.

I know Mark Jaggers' incredible life story. I know his unyielding quest for excellence. I've witnessed his ability to overcome what most of us would consider insurmountable odds. I have benefitted from his infectious enthusiasm and indomitable spirit. I marvel at his innate, natural leadership ability, both in the workplace and in athletic endeavors. God gives those gifts only to the very fortunate—or maybe in this case, to those who truly need the full measure of those gifts and who are strong enough to use them.

And did Mark ever use them! As a very junior officer, he worked directly for me while I commanded a US Air Force satellite operations squadron. His passion for the work and his constant desire to reach for the next challenge was evident from the outset. He knew that satellite operations were important, but he really wanted to fly Air Force airplanes. His beautiful wife, Becky, tolerated—if not encouraged—his desire to fly, and ultimately Mark was selected to attend the most selective of Air Force pilot training programs.

Not surprisingly, Mark excelled at pilot training and in flying the largest airplane in the Air Force, the C-5 Galaxy. He and Becky started their family, his Air Force career was progressing well, but then tragedy struck. Mark was diagnosed with a rare form of cancer, and despite surgeries and many other treatments, the best possible result was to merely hold it at bay and just live with the disease. A weaker person might have surrendered, but not Mark. He fought, but while he fought, he flourished as a person, a husband, a father. He just would not quit. And as many a medical person found out, he refused to accept no for an answer. He and his entire family had tremendous highs and incredible lows in fighting this awful disease—and due to the cancer, his Air Force career was finished.

Against all odds and all advice, he completed medical school as well as a residency in ophthalmology—while fighting the cancer! Saint Becky continued to provide Godly support to Mark and the family, allowing Mark to persevere and somehow coexist with the disease. The strength he showed, the pure grit and determination to succeed at both medical school and in the cancer fight, quite simply amazes me—and truthfully, it makes me feel inadequate.

But the story doesn't really end at those temporal things. Mark's faith in God, his abiding love for his family, and his concern for his patients all comes through in this book. And if there are things more valuable in this life than those qualities, I haven't discovered them.

Yes, this is a story of a remarkable man. I wish all readers of this book could share the privilege of knowing him. As you read the book, you'll gain some wonderful insights into his life and his personality, but no one word can adequately describe his strength, his passion, and his zeal for life. My life is enriched because I do know the subject of this book!

William L. Shelton

General, US Air Force

Preface
Winning and Losing

First off, why did I *have* to write this book? There were so many stories, events, and people involved in cataclysmic events, and they continually changed the course of our lives, I was afraid the details would become lost to the wind. This book is primarily for my family but especially for my children. They knew, heard or remembered bits and pieces of the story, and I wanted them to know the sacrifices so many made for us trying to restore our "normalcy." The feedback so far from them and many others, who were major players in these events, gave me a sense of accomplishment from this tearful two-month journey to collect my thoughts and place them on paper. Hopefully, it remains far beyond my life to help continually tie more people together, so more good comes from a tremendously difficult experience that has made me a richer and deeply appreciative man!

In our culture, we are intensely focused on the score in life. Despite living in a world of blended grays, we search out the distinct black and white to declare yes or no, with or against and yes, winner or loser. It is what we know and makes life more manageable for our simple human minds to grasp or own. We just wander aimlessly in the middle and feel lost. Our minds want absolutes. When someone dies from cancer, we talk about them finally losing their battle. I'd like to think about this winning and losing in a different context.

Possibly, it comes from the fact that I know at some point, my body will no longer be able to bear the burden of the cancer I carry. Thus, eventually people will talk about my valiant battle that lasted so many years. But why can't we feel comfortable in trying to live a beautiful life to the fullest extent our bodies, surroundings and most importantly our spirit, allowed us to live.

No matter what happens to me, I'll treasure my family, who nurtured me as a young man, helped me to believe in myself and run as fast as I can. Friends enriched the journey and filled in the branches of our proud, sturdy tree with vibrant memories. The Miller's traveled with us all over Europe where we dipped our toes in the Bavarian mountain streams, drank beers at Oktoberfest and tried to lose our very young children as they ran away from us in the streets of Florence, Italy. Mike, Bernie and Natalie Dahlem allowed us to join them on saddle and with paddle inside Yellowstone National Park where we discovered how tender our backsides were, especially Mike's. Endless soccer tournaments around the Midwest hardened our determination watching competitive soccer in wretched weather conditions, as our young children went from aimless players to skilled athletes. Golfing in Colorado became the ultimate in scorekeeping event. That is where Mike, Scot and I battled annually for a cheap piece of metal emblazoned with "Colorado Cup" just below its rim. The score is what placed your name on the prized possession, but it was the fellowship that really always brought me back. Of course, that is not to exclude the Colonel's hospitality and the purple mountain majesties just outside his back patio with its hot tub. All experiences with different people from various walks of life and too many others to relate here without writing another book. The beautiful memories we created together will be with me forever.

Read on from chapter one and remember these are real events pieced back together to the best of my recollection and research. I implore you to consider winning and losing in a different light. Live your precious life to the best of your ability and love those around you. In the end, it doesn't matter what the numbers count to, the people you touched and lives that are forever intertwined in meaningful ways are what truly defines winning. After all, if you believe there is more to all of this than what you see and feel in the present world, eternity is the ultimate victory and God isn't keeping score! He just wants to embrace your heart and soul!

~

I will be forever indebted to the numerous friends that took the time to read the rough draft of my story and gave their feedback. From Seattle, Barry and Jackie St. Germain had their own unique perspective and role in helping us deal with our mounting troubles during those darkest hours. Tim and Melissa Porter spent hours offering feedback and did significant research on how to pursue the possibility of publishing this work. Steve and Elaine Melonides in Chicago helped remind me of even more wonderful but forgotten stories, and the uniqueness of the human spirit. Father Dick Sullivan gave me guidance so I could try to deliver a message to anyone that chose to read my words might understand how deeply personal my journey became. Finally, to General William Shelton, who spent endless hours editing my work; his attention to detail was remarkable and I will be forever grateful for his time and expertise. Due to everyone's help, I feel blessed and hope a reader's time spent in reading this work will leave you a richer person for the experience!

Chapter One

A Hellish Firestorm

The whitish fog was slowly lifting, but the flurry of activity around me was unmistakable. Something really intense and wrong was going on in my life, and my mind was not clear. Was I dead or dying? "Oh God really!" Nothing seemed lucid enough to understand, but I can recall many people standing over me and urging any response to their barrage of questions. I was flooded with inputs but couldn't put the pieces together. I kept staring at a bright light, was I supposed to go to it? Too many question and no answers, at least for the moment.

~

Married to Becky, a wonderful, beautiful woman, I was living the dream. We had a blonde hair, two-year-old daughter, and a child on the way. I was a United States Air Force pilot flying missions all over the world. Our happy and healthy home was in Dover, Delaware, and I couldn't imagine a more loving environment. We were a long way from Jeffersontown, Kentucky where we both grew up. Sometimes, I needed to pinch myself when I looked into Becky's amazing blue eyes, wondering how we could be so fortunate.

Even though it had taken so much work to get us where we were in life, we still couldn't help feeling lucky. Somewhere in the back of my mind, I was convinced we had earned this position in life with a nice, new home in a pretty neighborhood, flying the largest airplane in the world, the C-5 Galaxy. Could any of this have also been due to God's grace? "Yeah, I guess so," is what I told myself, but only in fleeting moments when I wasn't busy living in this magical world. Besides, I had things to do!

In the fall of 1994, I was in Squadron Officer School (SOS) at Maxwell Air Force Base, Alabama. SOS was the mid-level management school for Air Force officers to get "repainted Air Force blue." We would spend about two months hanging out with a bunch of captains from other parts of the Air Force, learning history, strategy, management and leadership skills, as we prepared to move up the chain as Majors, Colonels and beyond. Hopefully, that is! I had just returned to Alabama after a brief Thanksgiving break to finish the course and I needed to get back home as quickly as possible, because Becky was due with our second child around the beginning of the year. Meeting officers from all corners of the world was fun, but I was tiring of some of the competitiveness everyone was displaying, because everyone wanted to be a distinguished graduate of SOS. It looked good on the resume' and helped in being promoted. I was certainly interested in that, as well, but I really wanted to get back to my wife, kid(s) and my life of flying airplanes.

Becky, the good soldier, was trying to keep a two year old busy in Delaware, while being eight months pregnant. Never an easy task, as she waited on me to return. The life of a heavy airlift pilot's wife was challenging, since we never really knew when I would be home. As world events unfolded, we would watch CNN and just wait for the phone to ring. Then, in the span of 24 hours, I would be placed on call to fly out into some God-forsaken land, where civil war, famine, or national defense needs, required our help. Unofficially, many of us called the 436th Airlift Wing the UN Air Force. Our daughter, Meredith, was oblivious to all this and only worried about where her latest pacifier was hidden. As we tried to wean them from her world, she had become the master of hiding those damn things. It was a tug of war to say the least!

Becky, being eight months pregnant, was ready to get her body back, but nobody is ever quite ready for the madness that comes with a newborn and the sleepless nights. Meredith certainly wasn't ready to share Mommy and Daddy. However, in the coming days, all of our lives were about to change in ways that we couldn't even imagine. Our son was about to be born into chaos, as a hurricane prepared to hit the Jaggers' house with a fury that would shake our foundation and our faith! God help us, literally.

~

December 1, 1994 is a date that has been burned into my cranium like an ugly scar, because it is the day that hell walked into my life.

The fog was quickly lifting now, as I looked up from my prone position at several faces looking down at me. I only recognized one of them, Drew, who was an SOS classmate. Several people were now dispersing, because the apparent emergency must have subsided, except now I was becoming fully aware that I was in an emergency room and lying on a gurney. Everything was white, except my green flight suit and the one worn by my buddy. Absolute panic set in as a whirlwind of thoughts and emotions filled my clearing head. "Oh, my God, I'll never fly again." A violent pinball machine was going off in my skull as I tried to figure out where I was and how bad was it. Something deep down inside told me that this was bad.

Drew, looked at me as I said, "What's going on?" He spent the next several minutes filling me in on the last half an hour that was lost from my memory. He went on to explain that I had shown up late for our initial briefing of the day in the "blue bedroom," which was the nickname of the auditorium where each SOS class spent hours listening to lectures and guest speakers. When I got there, I appeared lost, but also funny and belligerent at the same time. Normally, I'm a pretty courteous kind of guy, who understands when to shut up, but apparently not on this day. A group of officers from a different flight was sitting behind us and I was determined to be loud and obnoxious that morning. My flight members were getting a pretty good kick out of my newfound foolish behavior and willingness to taunt fellow officers in the blue bedroom. It seemed pretty funny for a while, as I turned around multiple times giving them grief while they threatened me with all sorts of disciplinary action. My flight crew was laughing, but theirs was getting angrier by the minute.

Finally, it became clear that this Captain Mark Jaggers was not the man that my flight members had met and been hanging out with for the past several weeks. Something was wrong. I was quietly escorted from the blue bedroom. Well, as quietly as I would allow it, that is. An ambulance was called and I was quickly taken to the base clinic for the emergency room staff to evaluate. My personal world at this point was fine, because I couldn't grasp a single moment of this adventure; that is, if you can call this an adventure.

The ER staff poured over me, baffled why an Air Force pilot could be so lost, and by now, almost unresponsive. Vitals were run and stat labs sent off before an answer came back that started to tell the story. My blood sugar was 29. The normal range should be 70-110 and I wasn't even close to the acceptable range. Immediately, D50 was given through an IV. This highly concentrated sugar solution is typically used for preventing diabetics from going into a hypoglycemic coma. The physiological response was rapid as my mind rushed back into focus and the questions being thrown at me were finally being followed by my answers. Within a minute or two, the D50 solution had brought me back into the world of the living, but now the questions were more troubling; why?!

I was moved to a different bay where I continued to talk with Drew about what had happened that morning. My mind was in full alarm mode, as I wondered what in the world would become of my promising career. The thoughts were so reckless, so fleeting that I couldn't keep track of them. My thoughts started going to what this would mean to my growing family. "Oh God, really, why now?"

Eventually, after the staff moved on to continue with their daily routine, the ER doctor came over to ask me several questions; most of which centered on whether I was an alcoholic or injecting myself with insulin. I looked at him as if he was from another planet. My only thoughts and answers were, "Are you crazy?" I was wearing a flight suit and had multiple medical flight exams done on a regular basis. Why would I inject myself with insulin, and I certainly wasn't an alcoholic. A possible answer, he offered, to why this happened was an insulinoma. A small tumor could be in my pancreas making insulin. Drew would go over to the library in the next hour to find out anything he could. At the time, the internet was still the toy of a small, technically savvy crowd and certainly wasn't mainstream. When he returned, I would voraciously read everything in his pile of research, searching for a quick answer that might put my world back together.

In the meantime, my flight was trying to figure out what had just happened. One of the officers in our group was an OSI agent. His real job in the Air Force was to do investigations on members suspected of crimes or misbehavior. Due to the very mysterious events that had just transpired, he took it upon himself to search my room, looking for drugs, legal or illegal, that might shed light on what was happening. Of course, he didn't find a damn thing, but I'm still trying to figure out if I'm mad at the intrusion into my life, since this guy turned my room into a crime scene. Of course, he was looking for any kind of an answer and I was just mad, confused and lost. It would get worse though, much worse.

I looked at the phone, wondering how to make the toughest call of my life. I needed to call my eight-month pregnant wife, who was home in our idyllic world, to tell her hell was on the way. I didn't really have many details for her yet, except that our Air Force life was certainly about to change, but I had no idea in what way just yet. My mind wasn't at full speed yet, and the phone number home almost seemed to come back to me in slow motion.

Becky answered the phone, and I can't even remember the details of the conversation, other than having a lump in my throat, as I held back my tears with all my might, and trying not to fall apart. I really just wanted to go home, curl up in her arms, sleep, and wait for this entire nightmare to go away. It wouldn't be that easy. She kept her composure on the phone and just reassured me that we would get through this together. Both of us probably didn't really want to let on what was really dancing in the back of our minds, but at least for that phone call, we kept it together. For now, she would remain in Dover, Delaware until we had a game plan. Certainly, to have a very pregnant woman jump on a jet with a two year old wasn't a great idea, but what other options did we have?

Over the next 24-48 hours, multiple tests were run with a focus on labs to see if this insulinoma was present. I prayed that they would find evidence of one. "God, let it be there so they can cut it out and let me go back to my life again!" However, nothing came back pointing us in the right direction. The medical staff at the small clinic was in over their heads. I knew it and so did they. I needed a regional Air Force hospital for them to figure out the puzzle, and I needed it right away. A C-9 flying ambulance was sent over to Maxwell Air Force Base to shuttle me over to Biloxi, Mississippi and Keesler Air Force Base's Regional Medical Facility. I packed my bags in my dorm room at SOS, said my goodbyes and was escorted to the flight line at night, waiting for the C-9 to arrive around 9 pm. No hoopla, sendoffs or family to give kisses; it was simply, "Good luck, captain," from the driver, as I walked across the dark tarmac to the steps of the jet. A nurse met me there and asked if I needed assistance. I didn't think so, but "What in the hell was going on?" raced through my mind and when would this nightmare end. I climbed up the steps on my own, wondering if I was flying into an abyss. I was so lost in my own head that I don't recall much of that flight, except for the constant vitals nurses were collecting from all the patients being flown to Keesler for care. No one on board could have ever guessed how empty my soul was that night. The only question that really mattered to me was when it would end. I felt panicked and paralyzed in the moment. Almost like a dead man walking. Problem was that it was closer to reality than I ever thought.

Chapter 2

The Beast Within

There are moments in your life when you are desperate to share and celebrate, and then there are others where you just want someone to be there when things seem to disintegrate. This was one of those times, because I'm not sure that I've ever felt so lonely. I arrived at Keesler AFB in Mississippi late at night with no welcoming committee again, just a bus ride from the C-9 over to the hospital to be admitted. Here it was the first couple of days of December and strange to feel such a warm breeze and watch palm trees sway as I walked onto the medical campus that was minutes away from the Gulf coast. The blackness of the night seemed so appropriate. It matched my mood. I was exhausted and a mess in this beautiful place. Honestly, I was desperate with hopes that they would find answers to put Humpty Dumpty's life back together again.

They gave me a room with another service member, and the next morning, interns and residents began their parade around the floor as they checked on patients. I was the puzzle that came in during the night, because no one really knew why this young, healthy 29-year-old pilot couldn't keep his blood sugar up. Pricking the end of my fingers became the ritual, as a regular schedule was instituted to document and to ensure, I didn't crash on somebody's watch. The young doctors came in, interviewed and examined me, promising they would keep me informed.

Another battery of tests was ordered. The constant needle sticks and ensuing wait were on!

~

At home in Louisville, Kentucky, my parents, LeRoy and Diana, had now received numerous phone calls and were well aware that something was seriously wrong with my health. They realized I was alone and made quick arrangements to drive down to Mississippi to be by my side.

This wasn't an easy task, since my father owned a general store in a rural part of Kentucky. It's just what you imagine from Mayberry. An old, white farmhouse converted to be a store with two gas pumps out front. Quaint, old and now with an oven installed, my dad was baking pizzas to keep the business profitable. And making damn good ones while at it! My mom was an RN at a very good local Louisville hospital, handling their quality assurance issues at this point in her career. Phone calls were made and accommodations handled. It's just the way it is in Kentucky. You help when called and expect or hope the same comes in return when you need a favor. We are all related in Kentucky, right? At least that is the rumor everyone seems to believe about the people in the south. My parents jumped on I-65 and started South with hopes they might be able to help in some way.

~

The next two days were spent worrying and catching up with Mom and Dad as test after test came back normal. The nights were becoming very interesting. I was being awakened every two hours for sugar checks, which makes for an ugly night's sleep, and on one night around 3-4 am the nurse assistant came in, checked my sugar, but left in a rush. In a matter of minutes, the lights were on and the intern, bleary eyed from being on call all day and night, started quizzing me like a game show host. I didn't know that Alex Trebeck was on duty, but the questions were rolling at a rapid rate. I finally had to ask what the fuss was all about. My sugar level was at an astonishing low of 16. Everyone was amazed that I was having this conversation, but I remember all of it, despite a blood sugar level that should have shut down my brain like a light. Quickly a bolus of D50 was pushed through my IV and multiple checks of my blood sugar helped put the crowd back at ease. The primary question was getting bigger and looming more ominous, since days of testing had produced no answers.

On December 5, 1994, a day, which will live in infamy, (sorry President Roosevelt for stealing your quote), the answer came. We had finally decided that imaging my abdomen was needed to see if the pancreas was abnormal. A computerized tomography (CT) scan was done with contrast that morning and I awaited the results.

~

Back home in Delaware, Becky was still waiting to find out what was going on and whether she needed to make some crazy plans for travel to Keesler. Being only three weeks from her due date now, pregnant women were not advised to jump on an airplane or they risked delivering a child on the way. None of that was ideal, so we prayed I could get some answers that would allow me to go home and get this speed bump in life behind us. Phone calls were made to friends around the country, but since we didn't have anything solid to share, everybody just waited.

~

I wasn't your typical patient, feeling like hell, stuck in a hospital bed and waiting to get better once the treatment or surgery cured the problem. I felt fine and wandered the halls trying to occupy my time. Inside, I was a wreck, but on the outside, I had to find something to keep my mind off the obvious reason why I was there. Waiting for the CT results, I happened to find the intern on duty that promised to keep me informed. He knew the question was coming, and yes, they went over the CT and had some things to show me. He was waiting for his senior resident to come back to the floor, and then they would come get us to share the news. Honestly, I was excited! For the first time in five days, somebody had some answers.

I went back to my hospital room, found my parents, and we waited for the doctors to deliver the findings. Not long, after sitting down, the intern came in and invited us to head to the doctor's conference room on the floor. The look on his face was stoic. I wasn't sure how to read him, but hey, he had some answers, and that is what I needed. The small, rectangular room was bright and had a table and chairs that filled most of its space. What is up with all these white, sterile spaces in hospitals! A reading light for looking at X-rays was on in one corner. We sat down, and the resident and intern sat across from us. It seemed as if it took forever to get to the point, but finally the intern strung words together that changed my world forever! "We found a mass."

Okay, so what does that mean was all my mind could really process. He picked up one of the films from the CT done earlier in the day and placed it in the reading light. It became obvious to this pilot's eyes that a very large "thing" sitting in the middle of that picture wasn't supposed to be there, and in fact, filled the majority of my abdominal cavity. My heart sank. "Oh, my God, really!" was what screamed inside my head, as shock and anger whipped together in a nasty mess. I sat there quietly, not quite knowing what to say. My mother was finally the only one in the room with the guts to say it, "Are we talking cancer?" The intern also appeared to be at a loss for words, but he finally uttered a simple, "Yes."

Fog filled my head, the room, the hospital floor and even Mississippi, as far as I could tell. We quietly walked back to my room. Rarely am I at a loss for words, but this moment was one of those times. My parents tried to console me as I sat down. I was too lost to cry. All I knew was that the world I lived in was now totally out of control, and I couldn't take any more inputs.

I honestly lost track of time, but at some point later, I needed to find the energy and words to make a phone call again. If I thought the previous call to Delaware was difficult, this Mount Everest sized task made the other one look like a molehill. The only things I can recall from that conversation was me saying the word mass, and Becky responding that she understood. The rest of that tape recorder in my head just seemed jumbled like Charlie Brown's teacher talking. We must have made some sense of the madness together, because the next day she was headed to her

OB/GYN's office for an exam to find out if she could fly to Keesler.

~

Becky had some very challenging decisions to make on what to do as far as travel and the care of our two-year old, Meredith. The OB heard the mess we were in, did an exam and confirmed that her cervix was not dilated and that travel on an airplane should be relatively safe. Whatever relatively meant? She made airline reservations for herself and Meredith, and they were on their way to Keesler to be by my side. Friends of ours from Dover AFB, in our neighborhood, agreed to keep an eye on our house for us until we could return. How could we ever dream that the house we built for our perfect little world, would never feel our presence cross its threshold ever again!

Chapter 3

The Battle Plan

Once the immediate emotions wore off, and we had become accustomed to something called a "mass," refocusing had to be the priority to figure out what was next. Blood sugar checks were routine now, and they even placed me on a low dose IV solution of sugar to help me try to avoid the night lows. Periodic eating during the night was also helping. Everyone I knew was stunned as news circulated around that I was really in trouble. My classmates at SOS even made a road trip to visit and they delivered the rest of my dorm room stuff and car. I had left there in the middle of the night, and they were finally able to reunite me with my things. Eventually, the SOS commander concluded that I had completed enough of the course to be given a graduation certificate. A generous gift, but considering what was going on in my life, I was no longer worried about flying, being promoted, or my next assignment. I had to find a way to survive against an opponent that didn't even have a name at this point.

~

Becky and Meredith arrived in Mississippi and with them came a breath of fresh air. Becky's presence gave me the sense of a toddler finding a security blanket, giving warmth and comfort to a chaotic situation. Both of us were numb, but we embraced and vowed to stick together through whatever came next. It was clearly a challenge that would push us to all limits. We found comfort in each other's arms. My life's teammate was there to help me absorb and digest information, while trying to take the next appropriate steps. Meredith was just the typical two-year old, which was good. Her future world's shape was clearly in the balance as well, but playing, saying "No!" and keeping us busy was what she needed to do.

As he built his young thriving law practice from scratch, my brother, Kevin, was now working on finding time to visit on the weekends. He would leave Louisville on Friday afternoons, joined by my dad, who was still trying to manage his store and pizza business. They would drive ten hours to Biloxi and stay until Sunday afternoon before making the return trip. Everyone was being worn down, emotionally, physically and now financially.

~

The doctors still couldn't put a name on this thing and in medicine, "tissue is the issue." A biopsy was needed to gather pieces to put on a slide so a pathologist could make a diagnosis. A pair of radiologists was scheduled to do the biopsy and I was wheeled down to their suite for the procedure. Becky accompanied me down the stark white halls and elevators; at least, that is how I remember them again. She gave me that gentle kiss I needed and I was delivered into the radiologists' hands.

Lots of equipment filled the room, and for the doctors to do their work, I was moved onto a firm piece of plastic, which they called a bed. My abdomen was prepped with a brutally cold, cleaning solution and a big blue drape was placed over me with a small hole in it where the radiologist were planning on doing their "drilling." I now experienced one of the more frustrating moments in this drama. The doctors arrived, said little if anything to me and started arranging their tools of trade. Eventually, I had several injections of numbing medicine placed, and then the real work started. Very large needles were being shoved into my abdomen, all in search of pieces from the mass. Well, the radiologists were doing their job and having one helluva conversation over the top of me, while I'm under this blue drape. The conversation clearly wasn't intended to include me nor help me understand what was going on. From what I could understand, they were mostly just getting blood from the biopsy samples. I was becoming very frustrated after being poked and prodded on for about thirty minutes. Some of it was very uncomfortable, as large bore needles were being passed through my fascia, the very tough lining that keeps your internal organs contained in the belly. I finally said in a very loud voice from under the drapes, "What the hell do you see?" After a brief pause, one of the radiologists just remarked, "It just doesn't look like any pancreatic cancer, we've ever seen." I had no idea of the significance of that comment at the time, but his words would reveal much about what they expected to find and about my prognosis. He was obviously startled by my presence and question. Maybe he needed to start remembering that some of his patients are awake when he starts doing these procedures! The rest of biopsy went without excitement, except for the annoying clicking noise created by the probe he was using to cut tissue from inside my body. I felt nothing with those subsequent passes, but being under two ice-cold physicians' care, surely didn't provide the warm and fuzzy feeling most patients are hoping for when they are scared to death. Fact is that I was scared to death. Eventually, I was reunited with Becky and shipped back to my room with hopes that bleeding wouldn't be an issue. Once again, the waiting game was on, but we were becoming professionals at this nasty game. Honestly, it just plain sucked.

It would take several days for an answer to come from the pathologists and the samples were also being shipped off to the Armed Forces Institute of Pathology (AFIP) in Washington D.C. for confirmation. This was obviously not the run of the mill kind of case. The beast was finally given a name. That name was a hemangiopericytoma. These tumors are known to secrete insulin type products, which certainly explained my blood sugar issues. This was a very rare sarcoma that is only diagnosed about 200 times per year, and I had to be one of the poor bastards with one. At least, it wasn't a pancreatic cancer. That almost certainly would have earned me a trip to Hospice for care until I died shortly thereafter. I was introduced to Dr. William Fox, the lead surgical oncologist at Keesler, and we discussed my case at length on several occasions. Treatment for this diagnosis is to cut it out. Radiation and chemotherapy were not terribly effective in handling this malignancy. He explained that if I were to have a chance to survive this hemangiopericytoma, it would certainly involve a major surgery, which could last around 18 hours by his estimate. Daunting task, but at least he felt as if he could handle it and Keesler's nursing staff was confident in his abilities. I was scheduled for the procedure the following week.

Here it was approaching the middle of December, and our lives were not only upside down, but now in the hands of a man I had just met. We had a game plan, but would it work and when it was done, what kind of physical shape would I be in as a result? Could I stay on active duty? Flying seemed so remote, but I always held out hope for the impossible. Would I survive the surgery or would Becky be a widow, Meredith fatherless, and my unborn son arrive into a world with a strike against him already? To say we were spooked would be the understatement of the year. Probably, for the first time in my life, I sat down, prayed that God help me, and I really meant it! Praying wasn't a regular part of my life. It wasn't that I didn't believe in God, I just couldn't figure out where he belonged in my daily routine yet. Now, I found myself hoping that God hadn't forsaken me and might find a way to help us as we struggled to deal with the last ten days, as we stood literally on the knife's edge.

Chapter 4
From Over to Under the Knife

We now prepared ourselves for a watershed moment that could release us from this mess or God knows what, if the surgery wasn't successful. Dr. Fox would make almost daily visits to my room to rehash the risks of such a large surgery. He meant well, but I was ready to get on with it! All the talking was just ratcheting up my anxiety level. I wanted to take the runway, push up the throttles, watch the afterburners light and see what happened when we pulled back on the stick.

One more major test was needed to help increase our chances of a successful procedure. Hemangiopericytomas are notorious for being vascular in nature. In other words, they are filled with blood vessels that can make resection very challenging, especially if significant bleeding is encountered. A resection is a procedure where a surgeon attempts to remove some type of tissue from the body. An angiogram was needed to map out the blood supply and hopefully some embolization could be performed. An embolization would help shut down blood vessels to the tumor in a safer way before my abdomen was opened and the risk of complications could become much higher.

Once again, I was sent down to my favorite white, sterile radiology procedure room for an interventional radiologist to perform the angiography and possible embolization. There were no major issues this time to cause me to blurt out angry questions from beneath the drape. I only recall a young physician, fresh out of his fellowship that looked overwhelmed by what he saw. It didn't take long before he just gave up and said it was too complicated and risky for him to attempt any embolization safely. The mass was like a bowl of spaghetti, and he couldn't figure out what any of the blood vessels were feeding. The ball was clearly in Dr. Fox's court now. Could he deliver?

~

Sometime in the early 70s, as a young boy around eight or nine, I can remember a moment that urged me to grow up very quickly. My mother, in her late twenties, had multiple health problems. She had survived a horrible car accident, lost a tremendous amount of weight and struggled off and on with addiction issues for several years. My brother was not old enough to understand what was going on, or the stress that her health placed on the household.

One very ordinary Saturday morning, I was watching cartoons like any other elementary school kid in America would. My mom was lying on the couch next to me, as I sat on the shaggy brown carpet of our living room in front of our brand new color TV. They were expensive, you know, and ours had arrived just in time for me to watch my beloved Dolphins beat the Redskins in Super Bowl VII for a perfect season. I was thrilled of course. Without warning, my mindless, color filled world was interrupted by a stunning question. My mother wanted to know, "Will you always love me, even if I don't get better?" I didn't know what to say, other than something any young son would offer. I told her, "I will always love you. No matter what, you will always be my mom." Inside, I was confused, but I wanted to give whatever comfort I could to a woman who appeared so weak and fragile, not just physically, but mentally as well.

Her health would wax and wane even to this day as she currently struggles with lung cancer, but I learned something about comforting others that day. It felt like I also grew up many years that morning. At that moment, my mother needed me to be more mature than my true age to help carry her when she couldn't find it in herself. She wanted unconditional love. Dad was a gentle soul, but for some reason, my mom needed her oldest son's acceptance, compassion and love. I gladly gave it; even if I didn't understand it at the time, and my mom would go on to encourage me as a teenager to become a man and to dream big. As far as she was concerned, nothing was out of reach for me. She didn't realize that inside I was feeling the need to grow up much faster than most kids because of her health.

~

As anyone can attest, waiting for a major surgical procedure really is probably worse than the procedure itself. At least that is conventional wisdom. I was turning out not to be conventional by any measuring stick. I wandered the hospital at Keesler looking for ways to keep my mind from worthless pacing, and the family just agonized over the 'what ifs'?

On December 14th or 15th, I don't recall or really care which, game time came and we gathered in prayer. Becky, Meredith, Mom, Dad, Kevin and Mike Dahlem were present. There were lots of hugs, kisses, and asking God if he could find a way to help us find success. Fear permeated the room. That morning, I took a shower using special soap to minimize the chances of developing a post-operative infection. All of us knew that this was a major procedure and dying on the table was clearly not out of the question here. I was wheeled down multiple hallways before Becky and my mother gave their last touch of love. I was too freaked out to even notice the white halls and frigid operating room anymore. Anesthesia couldn't start fast enough.

~

In the waiting area, everyone dug in for the long haul. They were told to expect an 18-hour surgery, so games, cards, magazines and naps were all at the ready or planned. Sometimes the best-laid plans don't seem to pan out though. In a horrific turn of events, Dr Fox arrived just one and a half hours into the expected surgical time with more devastating news. Hearts raced as only the worst outcomes could be expected at this moment. He went on to explain that he couldn't resect the mass because it was encasing one of the major blood vessels feeding many of the abdominal organs. If he attempted to remove the tumor and had a vascular surgeon help him reconstruct the superior mesenteric artery, I had a 50% chance of surviving the next several days. Too risky! He closed the wound and I was sent to recovery. A simple escape from the complex labyrinth was not going to happen. Everyone was distraught and tears flowed freely. Nothing seemed capable of stopping the downward spiral that prevented having our life back.

~

Once again, I peered from a foggy awareness, looking for answers in recovery. The first face I remember was Becky's wearing a forced smile. Whether I just pointed to my belly or was able to utter something like, "Is it gone?" I can only remember her response as tears poured down her face, "No." The nightmare just increased in magnitude to a level beyond anything I could understand. "Where was God?" I wondered as I slipped back into the mist.

Chapter 5

The Arrival

My time in recovery was uneventful physically, but mentally was another story, as Becky's due date loomed as well. It took several hours before I was fully able to grasp the failure at hand. Family members took turns seeing me, until I was finally sent to the floor for the next several days to try to heal as we regrouped. Everyone has seen the Wizard of Oz. I felt like I was in the spinning house with Dorothy, just hoping and praying that we landed on top of the wicked witch, with a chance of finding my way home.

The day after surgery was the moment I met the scar. As the nursing staff continued to collect my vitals, blood sugar levels, and administer medications, they finally removed the bandage that covered the surgical wound. "That is one helluva a gash," was all my mind could muster as the vertical and horizontal staples came into view, pinching my skin together from just below my sternum down to the pubic bone and then from that wound across on the right side of my abdomen for another ten inches. It was a massive wound into what I thought just one month ago was a healthy abdomen. For never having any previous medical problems or surgeries, I had jumped in with both feet and I was now the owner of a beast and a monstrous Frankenstein looking abdomen. I probably would have been more upset with the sight of those staples, except for the fact; it didn't appear as if they were going to matter much for the future.

~

In the summer of 1994, just six months prior, I knew I would be headed to the SOS course for several months. In between flying missions, Becky and I were trying to get as much stuff accomplished around the house as possible. She knew that taking care of our two-year-old daughter, Meredith, while seriously pregnant, would keep her from making headway with most home projects. We had just built a brand new home in Dover, Delaware so there was never a loss for things to do. One evening, we were rearranging furniture in the living room. The couch, a sleeper sofa, needed to be moved from one side of the room to another. That damn thing was made of lead and it felt just as comfortable. My job was to help move it with as little help as possible from her. Mission completed, but something was really killing me in the morning.

When I got to work at the Third Airlift Squadron, getting out of my car was excruciating. My abdominals were throbbing. I cursed that couch not so quietly and limped into work. I was determined to get into work as a C-5 pilot and executive officer for the Director of Operations of the 436th Airlift Wing at Dover AFB. It was becoming obvious though, that I was going to be headed to the most feared person on any air force base, the flight surgeon. Now, there was nothing wrong with our flight surgeons, but every pilot knows the doctor can end a flying career with one clinic note. I would almost hyperventilate when that annual physical came due. Years of training were always on the line when you went in for that visit and body cavity search. My arm would have to be falling off, before I would make an appointment outside of those required exams. All the flight docs I knew would bust their butts to keep you flying, but all of us knew the score. They had to keep the flying world safe and sometimes that meant grounding pilots when their health was outside of regulations.

I called the flight doc's office and had an appointment just before noon. Fortunately, my blood pressure, which always seemed borderline due to white coat anxiety, was fine and then the doctor arrived. He was friendly enough. After reviewing my chief complaint and hearing my story of moving a lead couch, he examined my abdomen. His remark was simple but repeated twice, "Firm abdominals." I had always prided myself in staying in shape. I worked out frequently and ran around fifteen miles each week. Being 29 with a reasonably flat belly was a real source of pride. He said I had strained abdominal muscles and sent me on my way with a script for Motrin to use four times a day. I was thrilled to leave his office without a major note in my record and went home to start taking the anti-inflammatory. Over the next week, the pain subsided, and I returned to his clinic, where he never examined me, but approved my return to flight duty. That obstacle was in my rearview mirror. At least, I thought it was.

Months later, I wondered what went through his mind when word filtered back to Dover that one of its pilots had a football-sized tumor in their abdomen and his life was hanging in the balance. Was he embarrassed or had he even noticed his miss?

~

We then started the play that I referred to as "Groundhog Day." Dr. Fox would come into my room on an almost daily basis and review my current medical status and recovery. Physically, I was coming along and I was fairly comfortable, considering the massive incisions made in my belly. His visits always ended with his thoughts about my future and they were dark discussions. A review of the current literature, and his experience told him that I had little chance of surviving the year, and no chance of making ten years. He repeated that message daily! I'm sure it was hard for him to share that news, but internally, it was crushing to my sense of hope. I truly felt that God really had abandoned me. The doctor kept giving me the same talk for at least a week. I guess it was because he was convinced I wasn't hearing it or because I wasn't showing enough outward emotion to give him the sense that the message was received. Well it was, but what it really screamed at me was that I would never walk my daughter down the aisle, see my unborn son walk, or grow old with the lady, who I promised a lifetime of love. Externally, I braced myself upright to get through the days, but inside I was a washing machine of emotion.

Elisabeth Kübler-Ross described five stages of grieving: denial, anger, bargaining, depression and acceptance. I went back and forth through all those stages, some of them at the same time, but always searching for any logical way out of this mess. To top it off, Becky was less than two weeks from delivering, and depression ravaged my mind. I couldn't come to grips with not being part of my new child's life.

I was given an indefinite pass from the hospital to live with my family in a facility next door to the medical center, as we made plans for whatever needed to be done. The Fisher House, we lived in, was a wonderful home built on many military bases with money from the Fisher family for service members and their families undergoing medical treatment away from their home bases. It was comfortable, pretty, spacious and new. It gave us a place to unpack our suitcases and gather our thoughts for a nominal price. Stress on the mass from the surgical procedure must have had some affect, because my nightly blood sugars weren't nearly as volatile. I only had to get up once a night to eat. I just wished that everything else could have calmed down.

As a family, we went down to the beach in Biloxi on Christmas Eve, forcing smiles and praying that 1995 would be filled with some answers. The warm breeze again felt so out of place to us and later the pictures we took, with palm trees along with the pristine, white sandy beaches, were a reminder of how out of sorts we were on the verge of January 1, 1995.

When we settled into bed the night before New Year's Eve, we had no idea that God would soon remind us how special the gift of life truly is. Less than a half an hour after midnight, Becky would wake me with not so gentle nudges; we needed to go to the hospital. Contractions had started and they were rapidly becoming more consistent and intense. Delivery was very near. Fortunately, we were less than a quarter mile from the hospital. We rushed to the car, and my dear friend, Mike, dropped us off at the front door. I'm sure things were dropping behind us as in an episode of, "I

Love Lucy," comes to mind. Mike had come down with his wife just to be there for us. While the rest of the family settled in for the night at the Fisher House, Mike used his jacket as a pillow on a typical, stiff hospital couch just outside our room. The anesthesiologist was on his way to give Becky her epidural, but was turned away by the OB who said she was too far along. She would have to do this natural. Rapidly, staff members were moving about preparing for the delivery as her contractions intensified. As any father would tell you, I felt helpless, but for the first time in weeks, I had no thoughts directed at my own personal health catastrophe. One of the greatest things in a parent's life was getting ready to occur and I was gleefully lost in the beautiful moment. Thank God!

Just one hour after arriving at Keesler Medical Center, it came to a crescendo as God gave us Colin Reed Jaggers. Initially, there were some anxious moments, because he looked like a blueberry, and the nurses quickly whisked him away, trying to make sure he was breathing. To make life more exciting, Becky was bleeding and the OB had a look that I had seen before. It didn't convey confidence. Fortunately, some well-placed sutures slowed the bleeding, and another crisis was narrowly averted. Colin had come down the birth canal so quickly, that his head never crowned. He was ready for the world. Whether we were ready for him was another question. A hurricane was still raging in our lives, but somebody upstairs had shaken me deeply. Something about more fight being left in that dog, as the five stages of grieving faded from my thoughts.

Once Becky had stabilized, Colin was pink and I was breathing again, I left the room with the biggest grin on my face to tell Mike, I had a son. He was stunned, expecting to be there all night on the hideous couch with the help of his make-do pillow. Unrestrained smiles were all around at 1:40 am in Biloxi, Mississippi. God had reached into my life and given me a gift again, which made me look around and reevaluate. The world looked different, my wife's face more beautiful and my daughter more amazing, as I finally realized this wasn't over. Only God knows when, and something told me all those gifts deserved all the fight I could muster. Welcome Colin Jaggers, and as for the "mass," well, game on!

Chapter 6

Finding Hope

The slow and steady recovery from surgery was still ongoing, but the battle for my own spirit and mind had clearly shifted in a positive way. Frequently, I would visit the hospital and see Dr. Fox to make sure the physical wounds were coming along. Groundhog Day was still the play of the month, but I was now emboldened with the energy to try to find any solution. I knew what was supposed to happen, but when I looked into all those blue eyes of my wife and kids, I found something inside that wasn't present on December 30, 1994. It was hope.

Cancer doesn't affect just one person; it affects a myriad of folks in your inner circle. My mother struggled mightily with all the news, which had so unexpectedly arrived with an ugly fierceness. Finally, she couldn't take it anymore and went to visit my surgeon without me being present. She broke down in his office asking him for any options he could recommend which might give us a chance to beat the odds. There could be no doubt in his mind that she completely understood his news and prognosis though. Her tears had left their mark. Whether he just felt sorry for her, my family, or me, he finally recommended an evaluation at the famed M.D. Anderson Cancer Center in Houston, Texas. He never wavered on what my prognosis was, but he did give in a bit by saying if anybody could offer novel treatments, Anderson was the place. My mom left his office grateful for his advice. Now the question became, how do we get there?

~

All of our worlds are full of mini-stories or chapters that define who we are and lead us down paths for better or worse. The most significant journey of my adult life really began in high school, where I met Becky. It certainly wasn't the straightforward love story people might expect and it would play out over almost two decades, but it truly defined my ability to be happy and to feel loved as a man.

During high school freshman gym class, new social circles began to coalesce, hormones raged and physical features began to emerge. Testosterone clouded the judgment of every young man and I certainly wasn't immune to its intoxicating effects. In the middle of this, I discovered a beautiful, skinny brunette with the bluest eyes I had ever seen. Their color was so intense, I wondered if they were somehow enhanced. I spent the semester eyeing her, but I was always too afraid to say anything. It wasn't until the last days of our freshman year in 1980, that I had the guts to say, "Hi!" and to eventually ask for her number. We planned a date to the Jeffersontown Four Theaters, just after school ended. Our first official date, and I admit that I was petrified. Little did I know that she was more scared than I was.

The theaters were close enough for me to walk to, but Becky lived in the sticks, so her mother had to drop her off. Being 14 created some real limitations on the dating scene. I don't remember the movie, but what became memorable was, "the move." Midway through the show, I found enough courage to try putting my arm around her. Bad mojo. As I raised my arm, I elbowed her square in the middle of her forehead and a difficult moment just became flat out embarrassing. The rest of the flick was strictly popcorn and soda. I didn't have the nerve to attempt moving my body, much less my arm. We left the theater, walked into the dark shadows near the entrance, and waited for her mother to arrive. It was late spring, and I guess love was in the air for me. Just as her mother pulled up, I threw out the fastest kiss any Kentucky boy could muster. It was a glancing blow and I was off to the races to walk home. Any thoroughbred at Churchill Downs would have been proud at my speed! Her reaction was stoic, as they drove away. I didn't see her again that summer and despite a couple of phone calls to her house, she never returned them. Great first impression and a huge strikeout!

We would spend the next three years as classmates at Jeffersontown High School, but we never mentioned that night ever again. In fact, there were times when we would double date. She would be with her boyfriend and I would be with my girlfriend. It wasn't necessarily awkward at this point, but our personal conversations were very limited. I was a basketball player and she performed on the dance team. We lived in different social circles. After graduating in 1983, we went our separate ways. I attended Purdue University on an Air Force ROTC scholarship to study Aeronautical and Astronautical Engineering, and she headed to Lexington, where she went to the University of Kentucky for business after spending her freshman year in Louisville at Bellarmine College. Periodically, we ran into each other in our small town just outside of Louisville, but the elbow to her head had probably knocked some sense into her, and she avoided future dates with me.

Four years later, our paths would cross again in a local drinking establishment called the Butchertown Pub. I had just graduated from Purdue and was waiting to head to Colorado for active duty, while she had taken a job as a marketing rep with a local company after finishing her degree at Kentucky. Something inside me stirred again as if I was 14. I saw those blue eyes and couldn't resist trying a second time. She caved and we started dating. The only problem was my future was out West as an Air Force officer in Space Command. It didn't matter this time around. I left in January 1988, and within months, Becky made the boldest move of her life by packing up and leaving for the mountains. I'm not here to say there weren't some serious doubts in my mind about how this was going to work out. In fact, there were times when I was frankly panicked that if it didn't, her family might be on their way to lynch a young lieutenant and my military career might be short-lived. Fortunately, after two and a half years of dating, it did work out. We were married at Saint Michael Catholic Church in Jeffersontown, Kentucky on July 21, 1990. We all remember that better or worse part, but who could imagine the ride waiting for two crazy kids who had just promised themselves to each other.

~

I spent the next several weeks filling all my waking moments with Becky, Meredith and Colin. Sleep became a premium for Becky as she dealt with a newborn. I took frequent naps as my body attempted to heal from the surgery. Incredible irony considering the fact that I could heal the surgical wounds with time, but the mass was also growing and filling my abdominal cavity. Something had to change or at some point, the game would be lost. I had stepped away from that reality for at least several days to enjoy being a father again. Colin went along for all our adventures. We visited the base playground on multiple occasions. Meredith hit the swings and slides, and tried to climb on all the different apparatus within the shadow of the base hospital. I carried Colin, whether I was supposed to or not, as Becky and I tried to immerse ourselves in the normal activities of new parents. Welcome diversions to say the least. Meredith was our daredevil and Colin the willing observer.

At some point in early January 1995, the focus had to switch back to making hard decisions. M.D. Anderson was clearly the best option on the table, and now I had to beg the Air Force to send me there for evaluation. That was no small task. Since I was an active duty member of our armed forces, my medical bills were the responsibility of the federal government. The problem is they have their own facilities, which they want to use, since it is much cheaper than being referred outside, "the system." The regional commander of Keesler Medical Center had to approve sending me to Houston. My ace in the hole was having such an unusual and life-threatening condition. His staff had admitted to me daily that they couldn't handle my problem. As negative as my surgeon was about my future, he somehow convinced that commander to relent and let me take an expensive paid field trip.

M.D. Anderson was very specific about what they wanted me to bring and payment from the Air Force had to be upfront. I assembled the scans, blocks of biopsy tissue and slides, lab results and surgical dictations that told the odyssey of procedures done so far. Homer's odyssey had nothing on me. They received a check for $2000 and would see me in the sarcoma clinic in the next ten days. I realized this was my best or possibly only chance to deal with the beast, so I was diligent in making sure they had whatever they needed for the consultation.

In the meantime, numerous friends came to visit and encourage us, as we also wondered what to do with our home back in Delaware. An incredible support network came together to help us meet needs as they arose. Another one of my closest friends at Dover AFB, Captain Barry St. Germain, became our steadfast lifesaver by handling any legal issues. He even drove our remaining car from Dover to Mississippi, since we had no concept when we might get back to the East coast. We had graduated from Purdue together in Aero/Astro Engineering and were fortunate enough to be reunited after seven years on active duty. He was one of the brightest people I had ever met and a good man. Other friends and family came to visit as well. When Captain Steve Melonides, one of my beloved Phi Delta Theta fraternity brothers visited, we tried to relax with a stroll around Keesler and talk about life. However, we couldn't ignore the intensity of the stress. Even the Spanish moss seemed to hang tighter and blow less carefree in the wind to me. To some degree, everything we did at that moment was somewhat forced or difficult, since nothing was certain or routine anymore. Again, some amazing irony as our walk took us down near the flight line and past the C-130 Hurricane Hunters squadron on the ramp. There would be no avoiding violent storms right now.

We were accumulating huge costs by living away from Dover. For the first time in my life, I had to seek out assistance from charities. It was a real slap in the face of our financial reality, as we faced a life-threatening illness with two small children. Retirement had now been mentioned more than once by the Air Force. That would mean losing half my salary, our home and career in a matter of weeks. If the medical nightmare wasn't bad enough, we now wondered where we might be living in the coming weeks. Difficult decisions were clearly ahead that didn't even involve the medical quagmire.

The kids were still blissfully unaware of how crazy a world they were living in at the time, but Becky and I both knew the Houston trip was beyond huge. Arrangements were made for me to catch a shuttle to the Gulfport airport, and then air transportation through New Orleans to Houston before catching another shuttle to a hotel near the Texas Medical Center. I left Mississippi in the darkness of an early morning of mid-January and arrived in Houston after an exhausting day. It probably wasn't that big of a deal to the experienced business traveler, but for a guy several weeks out of surgery and carrying around a football sized tumor, I was dead. I hoped that Houston felt otherwise about my condition.

The Houston Medical Center in 1995 was a maze of hospitals, parking garages, and clinic buildings. I arrived by shuttle and the staff met me to help orient me to my challenge. CT's, labs and delivering my goods had to be accomplished before I could meet Dr. Carl Plager. He was the physician in the sarcoma clinic, and in charge of evaluating my case. I had never seen such an impressive medical "world" as I experienced that day, but it was the staff that truly lifted my spirits. There was an attitude there, and it said, "Can!" I found myself in every waiting area with people from all walks of life in the same chilling situation. We were the worst of the worst cancer cases and we were sent to Anderson for hope. I expected nurses and phlebotomists to greet me with somber expressions. After all, they were caring for the walking dead. Instead, I found life and energy in those halls from the people who felt a calling to care for a desperate population. I couldn't help but walk with a bit more bounce in my step from the crazy mixture of anxiety, fear, and hope filling my head.

Dr. Plager was a very busy man, and I waited for hours to see him. In the long corridor, where his patients were held, there was one dire case after another seeking an answer to impossible problems. He would give his time to each and every one of us. When my time finally arrived, four hours after the scheduled appointment, he met me with a smile, and we went over each and every test. I'll never forget his dictation of our visit as he described me as, "A pleasant, young Air Force pilot." Why do I remember that? I have no idea, except that for the first time, I had met a doctor that smiled and engaged my case with the vigor of a much younger man. Outwardly, he conveyed a sense he could help. He was at least 60 years old, grey hair and balding, and after 45 minutes of evaluation and discussion, we had a game plan that included me meeting the Anderson Tumor Board. This was a multidisciplinary approach, where surgeons, medical and radiation oncologists would gather and have the week's most demanding cases presented. Fortunately or unfortunately, I fit neatly into that description. Patients sat in the adjacent hallway, waiting to be examined in a room in front of thirty doctors, if the board felt like it would be helpful. I was willing to do a song and dance of any type, if they wanted. After another long wait, I was called into the room.

At least two dozen doctors stared ahead as Dr. Plager introduced me to the brain trust. The chief surgical oncologist, Dr. Jack Gregory, came up to the front of the room and asked if he could examine me. Kind of barbaric and certainly not private, but I didn't care. I would have dropped my drawers in an auditorium if it helped, and I probably almost did back at SOS in the blue bedroom. I hopped up on the exam table, and he palpated my abdomen while examining the fresh surgical wound. He then helped me up and stepped back into the mass of featureless grey matter filling the room. Shortly thereafter, I waited in the hallway for Dr. Plager to deliver the news. My body shook inside when he told me the surgical staff felt like they could remove the mass and wanted to schedule me for surgery! I almost cried. God had given me energy through my family to keep moving forward, and now I had the top cancer center in the world saying they could help. I was stunned!

Quickly, I made my way back to the hotel, with no recollection of the shuttle, manicured grounds, or warm January breezes. I just needed to get news back to Mississippi that we had a chance. Hope filled our world again as I made my long journey through another set of shuttles, airplanes and bus rides back to Keesler on the following day. My family never looked so beautiful, and for the first time in weeks, I entertained real, unforced thoughts of being a father and husband again with a real future.

Chapter 7

A Chance

Excitement was running rampant around our suite in the Fisher House, back at Keesler AFB, as Anderson had delivered some seemingly impossible news. Parts of my mind still wanted to entertain being able to return to active duty, but I tried to temper those thoughts and keep my sanity. Meredith and Colin were still very busy being a two year old and a one month old respectively. Our toddler needed lots of attention and Becky's mom, Lois, was the perfect answer. She had come down to stay with us until the storm passed and her presence was an incredible blessing. Lois loved doing small artsy projects and this was right up the alley for a rambunctious toddler. The backyard of the Fisher house was full of pinecones, and it made for endless items to collect, glue and shape into all sorts of creations. The Southern pines delivered us lots of pine straw and material for Meredith's pleasure. Due to their young ages, I prayed that this mess would never be on their radar screen, or at least that is what I continued to hope.

Another major obstacle now stood between that surgery in Houston and me and that was the Air Force again. It became obvious on my return to Keesler that they wanted me off their medical liability care list. I was about to cost the system a bundle of money and in their eyes it was a lost cause. It took a week of lobbying the commander of the medical center to get him to consider sending me to M.D Anderson again as an active duty member. He made his case clear that I would be better off retired.

If I died, Becky and the kids would have lifetime benefits from the Air Force. That certainly was true, but it also meant I would go to Houston on Tricare and would be personally responsible for 20% of the bill. Retirement would also mean that I would immediately lose 50% of my salary. Our house in Delaware would have to be liquidated ASAP or just foreclosed to meet all the financial bills sweeping over us like a rogue tsunami. As much as I hated it, there was some merit to his argument. I called Anderson looking for advice. Talking directly with Dr. Gregory, who was the chief surgical oncologist at Anderson, and the one handling my case, he assured me I was not going to die on the table. He felt confident that he could remove this tumor. It promised to be a long and arduous task, but he was convinced the previous surgeon at Keesler was not prepared to handle the resection attempt and didn't have the best support network available around him to achieve a successful outcome. I was convinced and stood by my guns with the commander at Keesler. Anxious days passed as we tried to figure out what to do, if I was retired overnight. Financial meltdown was in our face.

Word finally came down through Dr. Fox. I would be allowed to proceed on active duty to Anderson. Fortunately, we were able to navigate that minefield and prepared to pack everything we had with us in Mississippi to head to Houston for the February 1, 1995 surgery. It was amazing how much stuff you can collect in just two months of living away from home, but throw in a toddler and welcoming a baby into the family-- our collection of belongings had become a mountain. A Bronco II and a small Plymouth Laser had to get us to Houston. With careful planning, we were able to put our collections in a U-Haul trailer and the cars for the next step in the journey. We left Biloxi around noon. There had been some very hard living for us over the previous weeks and a bright sunny day was a welcome gift and hopefully a positive omen. I had taken many bizarre trips in my life, but few that held my life in the balance.

~

Mogadishu, Somalia has one of the most gorgeous coastlines in the world, but in 1993, it was a world full of chaos. Warlords had taken over this country, which is literally on the Horn of Africa. Famine and death dominated the local populace as young men ran through the streets with automatic weapons, and rode in the back of open pickup trucks. It was the Wild West of my era, but in an African setting. The world was aghast at the daily suffering and loss of life and begged the United Nations to step in and help. The USAF found itself becoming the UN Air Force, as demands finally resulted in action. US Armed Forces, along with smaller units from other countries were sent to the region to stabilize the mess.

I had just arrived at Dover AFB to learn how to fly C-5's all over the world. Meredith wasn't even six months old when the Director of Operations of my squadron deemed me ready to be sent out on my dollar ride. In most airplanes that meant it was the first ride in an airplane and on completion of the flight, you presented your instructor with a decorated dollar bill. One side of the currency was usually inked up with a patriotic and macho theme, while the other side was frequently ruder. In the heavy airlift business, going out on a dollar ride just meant you were baggage for the rest of the crew and had no real responsibilities. Your job was to shadow the co-pilot and figure out exactly what he did. On the next trip, you would be expected to fly in his position.

My dollar ride was to head out with a crew to Cairo, Egypt and wait for the call to fly into Somalia with whatever equipment, supplies or personnel they needed. I was beside myself getting to go to a land I had read about in middle school, when I had even pondered becoming an archeologist like Howard Carter, hoping to find the next great discovery in the sands of the Sahara. We deadheaded, which meant we flew as passengers in the back of another Air Force plane, to the military airport West of Cairo. My skin tingled. After arriving in the middle of the night, we were shipped by bus to a four or five star hotel in the Giza area, the home of the Sphinx and pyramids, waiting for the call that we were on deck.

Our plush stay on the hotel's campus included clay tennis courts, swimming pools and endless buffets. I was starting to feel guilty about our accommodations. I was in the military and my first ride out into the world took me to a childhood obsession where I could sleep, eat, sunbathe and exercise while just waiting. I didn't want to tell Becky what the conditions were like, since she was home suffering sleepless nights with a baby. Unfortunately, one of my crewmates spilled the beans. Well, news travels fast. My next phone call home was dodgy.

We finally received news and a mission was cut to head to Ethiopia, where we would be closer to Somalia. Flying down the Nile River was surreal and I was glued to the windows. I loved geography and world history, so for me this was a dream. When we arrived in Addis Ababa, Ethiopia, a wildly diverse country of mountains, desert, canyons and plains was revealed. During that stay, I watched the sunrise from my window, while viewing CNN International as US Marines rolled up on the beaches of Mogadishu under the TV lights of reporters' cameras. Another bizarre scene and occurring just a couple hundred miles east of my climate controlled hotel room. After much discussion, it was decided that the elevation of Addis Ababa and its shorter runway would not adequately support our proposed mission.

We were shipped out to Aden, Yemen, which is on the heel of the Saudi peninsula. The only problem with that move was Yemen wasn't exactly friendly to US forces, and we didn't have diplomatic clearance to enter their airspace. I was too stupid to know any better, but my aircraft commander assured us that we could get them through long range or HF radio while on the way. Bad move. Leaving the mountainous region in Ethiopia and flying Northeast took us across eccentric African landscapes, you could only imagine in a science fiction movie. Upon reaching the coast, I was in awe of the size of the world. To the North, I looked upon the mouth of the Red Sea, which separates Africa from Asia. Something about Moses percolated up in my memory. The sea was a thousand shades of blue as we looked northeast and spotted Aden off the nose. The HF radio was ridiculously worthless in this region of the world, and at that time of day. Our gamble failed, and we couldn't obtain diplomatic clearance, but voices over the short-range (VHF) radio were friendly and welcomed us to Yemen. The crew seemed relieved. We went through all the flight checklists as we descended into and landed in Aden.

On the ground, our mood changed quickly as a jeep full of Yemen military officers ascended the stairs with a confrontational attitude, and wanted our commander to go with them. They wanted somebody's head. As the newbie, I wondered if this mission was standard fare or just an unusual turn of events. The aircraft commander left the aircraft, wide-eyed, as he climbed into their jeep. He was whisked away to a far corner of the airfield. We were left waiting to find out if we needed to leave in a rush or unpack our bags. He returned about an hour later with an ashen face and told us their military had supposedly locked us up on missile radar during our approach, since we didn't have diplomatic clearance. They didn't take a shot, because on the previous day, an Air Force C-141 had arrived with the proper paperwork. They figured there must be a mistake somewhere. Whether this story was an exaggerated truth or complete falsehood, we weren't anxious to stick around and find out. We prepared the jet for departure. The airfield denied us any services, so we only had whatever gas we brought with us. Fortunately, we had planned lots of extra fuel, but our options for airfields that could support our massive airframe were limited. During a landline call to Saint Louis, our command authority for the mission wanted us to proceed to Cairo. We were willing to comply, but when we left that airfield just 72 hours before, they didn't have lights, and night operations were prohibited due to a horrible visual illusion that had killed several aircrews over the years. They assured us the lights were now operational. If we headed to Cairo, we wouldn't have any gas to divert a significant distance, so this had to work. We closed the doors and got the hell out of Dodge.

Our trip to Cairo was routine, until we approached the destination. It was now four AM as we made contact with the military controllers. We were informed that the field was closed due to lack of lights. After a long and difficult conversation, Cairo West refused our request to land. Cairo International was our only reasonable option and the Egyptians were adamant about not letting our big plane land there and take up space at their civilian airfield. Declaring an emergency fixed that problem, but also upset the locals to the nth degree. A landing was made and now we needed to find lodging. Another problem; we didn't have civilian Egyptian Visas in our passports. St Louis told us we would be okay and urged us to hide our firearms on the jet and proceed through customs. Mutiny was just about to occur as the crew was now "helping" our young aircraft commander make better decisions. We opted to do an emergency extension of our already 24-hour duty day and wait to take off at sunrise, so we could land at the military airport. After two more excruciating long hours of sitting around, we lifted off with more gas and flew five minutes west of the city, but not before making some breathtaking passes over the Sphinx and pyramids with the sun just breaking the horizon. An amazing end to a strange day. The next day, St Louis gave the exact same route to another crew, but they elected to go through customs in Cairo. It took the US Ambassador to get them out of jail.

I have seen some freakish things in my life. Though nothing could have prepared me for the madness and stress, my health would put us through in the coming years!

~

The trip through Southern Mississippi and Louisiana was uneventful, but our minds were way ahead of the vehicles carrying us. Social workers had provided us with lists of long-term housing options to minimize the financial burden. There was no almost free, Fisher House close to the Houston Medical Center. We had to find something affordable, since it was likely that many of us would be there for the foreseeable future.

A maze of highways met us as we approached the city from the north, and despite arriving at what we were certain was not rush hour, highway 59 was packed with motorists and massive construction. Growing up in Louisville had not prepared us to deal with this crazy traffic, but we found our way to the medical center and the nearby Holiday Inn. Many issues still needed to be handled, but we had made it. We refused to admit our anxiety to each other, but hope also permeated our group as another major surgery awaited in the next day or two.

January 31st arrived and I was checked into the hospital for blood sugar management the night before the surgery. Whatever stress the previous procedure had created on the mass was now waning, and my nightly sugars were becoming an issue again.

Couple that with not being allowed to eat during the evening hours and cleansing out my bowels with colyte, I had a pretty rough night. The bowel prep seemed worse than any aspect of the surgery, because you couldn't decide to sit down on the toilet or stand since it was coming out of both ends like a water hose and just as forcefully. D50 once again came to my rescue in the middle of the night, and my sugar was restored for the rest of the evening.

The morning brought my army back to the bedside, as we anxiously looked forward to round two. This time around, our confidence was stronger, due to Dr. Gregory's reputation and encouragement that this would go well. God had brought me this far, and my faith was still discovering a sense of self, but hope was a welcome feeling next to the fear I still couldn't shake. No special soap was needed to wash my skin this time. It was simply wear this gown with nothing else and let's go. Hugs and kisses went around the room and I was sent off. The deeper into the hospital we went, the more sterile and cold it became. I remember it vividly, because no anesthesia had been given yet. Waiting first in the hallway outside of the operating room, and then inside was a stark reminder of the foreign environment I was in. Finally, with great relief, a face appeared above me with an oxygen mask, as he asked me to count down from 100. I remember maybe 97 before…

Chapter 8

Climbing out of a hole

Everybody settled into the surgical waiting area at MD Anderson. There was an eerie sense of déjà vu, but nobody was outwardly willing to discuss that possibility. Becky, my parents and brother, along with Mike Dahlem, were trying to find ways to keep themselves busy. They were once again promised a very long day, since Dr. Gregory also figured that it would likely take the team of several surgeons 12 to 18 hours of work to remove the hemangiopericytoma from my abdomen. To handle any and every surprise, he had collected over 60 years of experience for this effort. Collectively, everybody held their breath and brought out the cards, magazines and games again for the long haul.

"You've got to be kidding me!" was probably the only response the group could muster, as surgeons appeared looking for the Jaggers family, just one hour into the surgical start time. I was bleeding, and they were struggling to get the situation under control. They assured everybody that all actions were being taken to stabilize things, but the attempt to resect the tumor was over, and they were now in full evacuation mode, just trying to keep me from croaking on the table. "What happened?" was the recurring question, but at that moment, the staff was not willing to give many more details than they already had. A devastating shock wave hit that corner of the waiting area, and now, panic was the only thought readily available. The clock now ticked as if it had been soaked in molasses and minutes truly turned into hours. Pleas for updates were met with blank looks, because nobody outside of the operating room knew what had or was currently happening. Was I dying? There were no answers for hours.

~

Down in the depths of the hospital, the surgeons were frantically trying to get out of my abdomen. Uncontrolled bleeding was threatening my life. As the initial incision was being made through the original surgical scar, the tumor was violated along with scar tissue that had formed between that wound and the tumor capsule. Hemangiopericytomas are vascular tumors. Now, everybody was seeing first-hand how vascular, as blood filled the surgical field, and desperate hands were trying to plug the dike. Multiple attempts to pack the wound were only partially successful.

~

Little information flowed from the surgeons to my family in the passing hours, despite numerous pages overhead. Only the worst news could be imagined, as everybody braced for what came next. Hours later, the surgical oncologist fellow studying under Dr. Gregory finally found the family and explained that I had been transferred to the surgical intensive care unit (ICU) just about one hour after the start time of the procedure. Once the bleeding started, their only option was to get out and to stabilize me. I had been packed to help stop the blood loss, but my wound was open and fluids and blood were being transfused quickly to make sure my blood pressure didn't drop and cause brain damage. Clearly, I was not doing well, but at that moment, I was not dying. Dr.

Gregory had disappeared like a ghost, and hours later when my mom and Becky were finally able to find him, he was a shaken man. The bravado had been lost. He looked like a surgeon that had come perilously close to losing a patient on the table.

~

In the ICU, I was still bleeding and over the next 24 hours, I would receive 30 units of blood along with various fluids. My body was severely swollen and I looked like the Michelin man. Becky would stay by my side as the ICU staff worked the IV medicines and pumps feverishly until I was taken back to the operating room on the following day. They needed to remove the packing to see if the bleeding had finally ceased. I was so swollen at this point that the wound couldn't be closed in a traditional way. I would have to heal by secondary intention. That meant tissue would have to granulate into the gaping abdominal wound over the coming weeks and months, since traditional closure was impossible. Hemodynamically, blood pressure and fluid management wise, I was finally stabilized and shipped back to the ICU for recovery.

Over the next week, I was at a minimum a disruptive patient and at times even violent. I yanked out IV and A lines, screamed at staff, all the while demanding Becky. She had to be exhausted from the constant pull in so many directions. Our young kids were hanging out with her mother in a nearby hotel, while her husband had lost his mind in the ICU after a near-death experience. I don't remember a single detail of that week. I was too drugged to be aware, but certainly not quiet.

~

A strange thing happened to Becky while in that hotel suite though. It was late at night, she was climbing the stairs and an upstairs TV was on some type of Christian show, like "The 700 Club." When she went over to turn off the TV, one of the hosts had her eyes closed and was praying softly. Her message was for somebody in the audience to know that the bleeding going on in the belly of a friend was going to be okay, and that they would be healed. Becky was dumbfounded. She found her mother and shared what she had just seen. Then the tears broke through her defensive wall and flooded her world. At that moment, it was as if God was speaking directly to her!

~

The constant rocking and shifting cargo inside the covered wagon kept me awake as I begged the people around me to turn around for Houston. They ignored me. I watched them play games and speak Spanish while eating meal after meal. There was no suspension system and every bump just caused the pots and pans hanging above my head to just clang louder. We stopped frequently along the road, but they wouldn't let me leave. They weren't physically restraining me, but I had no idea where I was. I felt powerless in some kind of kidnapped state. Finally, after what seemed weeks in this covered wagon, they turned around, let me go and I awoke in the ICU. My mind scrambled back to reality and out of this dream world to see that I was still alive and being transferred to the regular floor, after seven very difficult days in the ICU. Hallucinations had filled my empty mind with bizarre images and thoughts, possibly in a way to protect me from the extremes my body was experiencing.

~

Back on the floor, I struggled to regain control of my body, mind and life. I was so weakened by the failed resection attempt that I had trouble just making one lap around the nurses' station. My family and I almost came to blows in the bathroom, since I was determined to clip my nails. I stood in front of the mirror with my legs shaking wildly and on the verge of collapse. In a simple act of defiance to what was happening to me, I was going to do this small task and do it myself. Everyone pleaded for me to sit down before I fell. "No," I was determined to get things back on my terms and finish clipping my nails. My stubbornness was in full glory for all to see.

Over the next three days, I didn't sleep one minute. My mind was so wigged out that I couldn't think straight and sleep seemed an impossible task. Maybe I was afraid of not waking up or just overwhelmed with the medications used to get my body through the past week. The family took turns babysitting me and trying to help me be as comfortable as possible. The days were filled with painful wound dressing changes for the fresh insult on my belly that wasn't fully closed. Gauze was pulled out and replaced daily in an effort to keep it clean, while tissue granulated in to fill the wound. It hurt like hell and looked even worse. Fortunately, my mom's nursing skills were well suited for this care, and she taught everybody how to step in and change the dressings. Nightly hot and cold flashes kept me from ever being very comfortable. My brother would sit there for an eight-hour shift trying to read one section of the paper, while using another to create a gentle breeze for me when I started the night sweats.

One of the more amazing stories came from one of those nightly babysitting periods. My brother and father were responsible for looking after me during those first few nights when I couldn't sleep. Dad would curl up on a stiff chair that reclined in the corner. Kevin, the night owl, took that opportunity to catch up on his reading with the use of small light. The room was otherwise still and dark, except for the occasional beeps from the IV pumps or monitors. I tried to sleep, but spent most of the night staring into space, hoping at some point that I would just pass out. When I started sweating, I urged Kevin to swing the paper back and forth faster, hoping to cool my body. In the middle of this surreal scene, LeRoy sat up and wondered where the breeze was coming from. In that dark corner, he reached into his pocket and found his cigarette lighter. A couple of turns on the wheel and voila, a one or two foot flame emerged from his little device. Immediately, several four-letter word barrages were thrown at him from Kevin and me and the flame quickly disappeared. We verbally disciplined him for the next several minutes as he stated, "I just wanted to know where the breeze was coming from." Well, in an oxygen rich environment and with a patient on oxygen, he had just tried to blow us all up. I could only imagine the headline in the Houston Chronicle the following day: "Patient survives cancer surgery, but dies from massive explosion." We laughed later, but at the time, LeRoy was taking it on the chin from his boys. Finally, three days after leaving the ICU, I found sleep, and this time without riding on a covered wagon or eating burritos.

Several more friends arrived in Houston to see if I was okay. Frank and Tim were also close fraternity brothers of mine from Purdue, and they were a bit stunned to see me in this shape. They helped give the family a break and at times just sat at the end of my bed quietly. Their presence was very comforting. I just longed for the times we had together on campus with few worries except how to pass that next test or find the next beer. Things were simpler back then.

~

I opened my eyes and found with great amazement numerous stories written on the tiles above my bed. Messages from grateful patients who were saved at Anderson, along with long chapters from angry people who were losing their battles with cancer and had since died. They cursed the place and the room I was currently lying in. I couldn't take my eyes off all the messages and tried to take in everything people had written. Frank, sitting next to the bed, finally asked me what it was that I was seeing and whom I was talking to. I tried to explain to him all the stories written above my bed in the textured ceiling tiles, but he looked confused. I was frustrated with his inability to see what was so obvious. He simply couldn't see what wasn't there. Hallucinations were still haunting my mind. I struggled to put all the pieces back together under all the physical and mental stress.

~

After seven more days, I was discharged from the hospital and went to the hotel where Becky, her mother and the kids were staying. Dressing changes, although gory, had become routine. I took frequent naps throughout the day, but Becky didn't get that lucky in trying to entertain or care for the kids. That task was taking its toll on her. We did make frequent walks next door to a small, family run amusement park that had horses. Meredith was always thrilled to ride "Old Smokey" around the barn as Colin took it all in from the stroller. This was a nice diversion for us as a family, but we needed to find some stability.

Keesler was now hot on my heels to process the retirement paperwork as quickly as possible. They were almost right; I had just about died on the table. Financial costs were driving them to get me off their plate, because that failed resection attempt, ICU and hospital stay had cost them a bundle. I relented and asked Barry St. Germain to put our house up for sale ASAP.

We prepared to leave Houston and go back to Louisville. I was too weak to spend 20 hours in a car, so I flew back home with my mom. During layovers, I would find some carpeted space in the airport to lie down and rest my broken body. Becky, Meredith, Colin and her Dad repacked the cars, rented a U-Haul again and made the long drive back to Kentucky. Dr. Plager had given us some guidance on the chemotherapy regimen that he felt gave us a 30-40% chance of shrinking the tumor. He held real optimism for the treatment plan he proposed and thought it could still help me. It was our job to find a facility for me to receive it. He would help in any way possible and see me every three courses of treatment to see if we were on the right pathway. We stumbled back to Louisville, where we finally decided to let the medical oncologists at Wright Patterson AFB administer the drugs recommended by Dr. Plager. By this time, though, we were clearly struggling to put one foot in front of the other!

Chapter 9

Shrinking Away

Gathering back in Kentucky with family and friends gave us a chance to heal and catch our breath. We were headed to Wright Patterson AFB since they had a Fisher House for lodging, and it was a regional Air Force medical facility. That meant they would have a large collection of physicians, equipment and facilities to handle my chemotherapy. I was also still on active duty, but on temporary leave, as my retirement was now just a matter of time and paperwork. Dayton, Ohio was two and a half hours from Louisville. Not ideal, but at this point, we had to make the best decision, given the circumstances.

Word was now reaching our various groups of friends. The response was humbling. In Louisville, our high school classmates, led by David Ratterman, organized a fundraiser at a local pizza pub. His band played free, and a portion of all money spent that night was donated to us to help with all our expenses. I had been back in Louisville for about a week and couldn't decide if I could go and face all those folks, physically or emotionally. I eventually chose to attend at the last minute and was stunned by the outpouring of love. I had not seen many of those people in 15 or more years. Inside I struggled to keep my composure, but outside a smile found its way to my face for the first time since the Houston debacle. I couldn't imagine how I was worth this display of humanity. God was good! I was still working on the faith thing, but the pace of the wrecking ball in our lives was so great, I hadn't really given it anything close to its just due. I told myself quietly that I would. Despite the obvious signs in my life, I was looking for excuses at this point to do anything but hard thinking, and faith was a partial casualty at this point.

Tim Porter knew that he also wanted to do something. Honestly, he may have one of the kindest hearts I have ever encountered in my life. Tim sent out letters to all our fraternity brothers, sharing what was going on in my world and asking for donations. Responses poured in along with checks. I was stunned.

My closest friend, Mike Dahlem, who lived in Louisville, shared the message of need as well, and again checks arrived on my parent's doorstep. His sleepy puppy dog eyes hid a shrewd business mind and a deep desire to help in any way he could. I knew we desperately needed assistance, but a part of me struggled to accept what was being given. Whether I was embarrassed or still convinced that I couldn't be worth all this effort, I couldn't bring myself to cash the biggest checks. People would ask if I received the money, but I just didn't know what to say. I was so grateful, but also so lost. I pray to this day that those people could somehow understand how precious those gifts really were even though I never cashed many of them.

An army had arisen around me and I could honestly feel the energy. My body was still recovering, but I was ready to get back up on my feet and start treatment. By March of 1995, we moved up to Wright Patterson and settled into their Fisher House. It was basically a converted duplex in family housing. There was a fairly large common area, but our room was the size of a small hotel room. We had our own bathroom and a microwave, but little space for a family of four to live in with a toddler and a newborn. When the play crib was set up, we were literally crawling over each other and the beds to get around the room to open drawers. It gave us a place to close our eyes, empty our bags and sleep at night for almost no cost, and it was next to the medical center. It would have to do.

My new medical oncologist, Dr. Johnson, was willing to use any treatment formulation M.D. Anderson and Dr. Plager came up with for my care. A new problem presented itself; the wound that Anderson couldn't close traditionally during my last surgery had partially dehisced or reopened all the way to the tumor, creating a one-inch hole in my abdomen, just below the sternum. This complicated matters, since it would have to be packed and changed on a daily basis now. It set the stage for a possible infection when my blood counts plummeted from the aggressive chemotherapy that was coming. I knew my hair was going to fall out, but I really didn't care. The barbershop seemed a bit stunned when I showed up and said to shave it all off. Once again, I wanted to control something in my life, and this was a small but important gesture that I had some control still left.

I was admitted into the hospital for the weeklong continuous infusion of four different chemotherapy drugs. For six days, I walked around the halls pushing an IV pole with two or three pumps attached to it and the drugs hanging above. The worst of them was Adriamycin. Some patients referred to it as the "red devil" due to its nasty side effects. I was supposed to get a hefty dose of it, since studies had shown it was the most effective medication available to shrink sarcomas, the general category for my mass. Dr. Plager had told me that my best chance for success was to receive very high doses of these different agents, since I was generally healthy outside of having a football-sized tumor. Say no more, I was willing to do anything to increase my probability of success. We were also warned that when my blood counts plummeted about two weeks after treatment, my risk of infection would increase and any fever could be a sign of impending disaster. I had to seek immediate care or risk dying in a matter of hours or days from an opportunistic infection.

Slowly I noticed my interest in food waned, but I wasn't terribly nauseated initially. They kept me pretty tanked up on medications to control that issue. Before long, though, the many smells of the hospital started to bother me. Everything from the wax on the floors, cleaners in the bathroom, but most importantly the tops that were placed on the food from the cafeteria, became almost unbearable. Frequently, I would stop the person bringing dinner at the door and just tell them I wasn't interested. Picking up that dark plastic top over the food plate unleashed trapped smells, causing my stomach to tumble. It seemed like I could smell every piece of fish, steak or spaghetti that the top had ever covered. Soon, I was mostly on a self-imposed liquid diet and trying to choke down a can of Ensure or Boost to increase my protein intake. Pounds started melting away at a fairly rapid rate.

The first round of chemotherapy went well, except for the eating thing, and I went back to the Fisher House, waiting for what was left of my hair to fall out and blood counts to drop. Fortunately, the kids stayed healthy, which was good for them and me. Lots of naps and Tylenol were needed, because at times, it was as if a truck ran over me for the first several days after treatment.

Our daily life was pretty boring and routine taking care of the kids. Early on, we made sure to visit the Air Force Museum. It truly has the second greatest collection of flying machines anywhere in the world, only behind the Smithsonian's Air and Space Museum, in my opinion. Meredith was much more interested in running around and Colin was starting to giggle with delight at her mischievous behavior. For an aeronautical and astronautical engineer, the X series planes were an amazing look into some of the greatest years of flying and engineering's transition from propellers to jets to hypersonic planes/rockets. As any young parent can tell you though, you have a brief window of opportunity to keep a child's attention, then you just have to move on. Walks highlighted most of our daily routine with the kids around base housing and swings on the playground in the Fisher House backyard.

As promised, on about day 20 from starting chemo, a visit to the bathroom reminded me of some of the effects from the drugs. As I started to urinate, a handful of pubic hair announced that this would be the day my hair started to go. How could I be stunned, you might ask. I'm not sure, but my mind never put two and two together that this meant pretty much all your hair. Eyebrows, lashes, hair on my legs and arms were not completely immune and before long, I was almost completely hair free. The residual nubs on my shaved head eventually went as well. For a while, it was pretty interesting putting pants on in this hypersensitive kind of state.

Blood counts were also being taken about once a week to see when and how far I bottomed out. A phone consultation between Dr. Plager and Dr. Johnson resulted in her receiving a bit of a spanking. Anderson wanted max doses for max effects, and she didn't order frequent enough labs to see my true nadir. It appeared there was still enough room to jack up the doses for the next round. Dr. Johnson agreed to follow Anderson's guidance much closer this time around.

Three weeks after the first round, I reentered the hospital for another long week of drugs. This one found an overanxious surgical resident that was very interested in the fistula, the opening in the incision that had formed on the midline incision just below the sternum. We had been changing its dressings on a daily basis, but he thought it needed to be debrided. After removing the gauze, he shoved his index finger into the hole as if he was digging for gold. He found more than what he bargained for that day. What happened over the next several minutes was frantic and ugly.

A one-foot high vertical eruption of blood emerged from the fistula. This young surgeon was clearly startled as he literally plugged the hole with his finger and screamed for help from down the hall. He was scared. Rapid thoughts were tossed about in my head; I really wondered if this was going to be the way I died. I kept calm as numerous physicians and nurses now filled the room. The surgical resident was now white and asking for lots of gauze to pack the wound. His superiors were instructing him on the next steps. I demanded that a phone call go out to Becky at the Fisher House to tell her to get to my room now. The tension in the room was clearly evident on every face, but as the packing went back into the fistula, the bleeding slowed and finally stopped. I was pissed. "Didn't you read my surgical report from Anderson? This thing is vascular. Don't mess with it," were my only thoughts. Fortunately, I never said it out loud or they probably would have sedated me. I was headed to the ICU for close monitoring over the next 24 hours and to make sure I had stabilized.

Fortunately, there were no further problems from that adventure. Becky made it to my bed, to make sure I was okay. In the morning, I was still amazed I let the guy touch me again. The resident came over to remove the packing, but this time with his attending looking over his shoulder. I must have been nuts to let him change the dressing, but I did and no bleeding was encountered. Lesson learned *again*; don't mess with this thing. I was sent back to the floor and I continued the chemotherapy.

The smells on the floor once again became my focus as my appetite waned even more. I was urged to eat as much as possible, but I simply wasn't interested. Pounds continued to disappear, and I wasn't somebody who came in with much to spare. I tried to ingest anything, but what mostly worked were sugary drinks, candy bars and desserts. Little protein existed in my diet. I was discharged back to the Fisher House, and we repeated the cycle of walks, swings on the playground and labs. Except this time, labs were drawn almost daily, as Dr. Plager wanted.

~

Paperwork finally caught up with me in April of 1995. I was officially placed on the temporary retirement list, as the Air Force waited for me to die, stabilize, or improve. It cost me half my salary, but at least I had medical benefits. Barry St. Germain came out from Dover AFB along with our Squadron Commander, Colonel Nelson, to complete the simple ceremony. They also brought with them around 40 large green canvas "A" bags, filled with gifts. It was another poignant moment that reminded us how special our flying community was. I elected to keep the retirement casual, since I couldn't wear my dress blues, due to my protruding stomach and all the wound dressings. The few pictures that remain from that event reflect a somber time and show an officer standing by a good friend and our commander with our heads down. Dover AFB now knew the extent of my trouble and they must have wondered how long before a death notice came across the wire.

Barry was an absolute lifesaver, because he had put our house in Delaware up for sale, maintained the yard, cleaned and packed the house and finally sold it to an incoming pilot and his family. Christmas was coming when Becky jumped on a plane for Biloxi so decorations, a Christmas tree, lights and presents were still on display. Barry and Jackie, who was pregnant with twins, took on that additional duty as well to make sure everything was put away and those presents eventually found their way back to us. They went so far above and beyond, we could never quite find the words to appropriately express our deepest gratitude. The house that I left after Thanksgiving, and Becky left in early December, was now gone. We were so fortunate to have Barry and other families from the squadron to care for our things. It saddened me greatly that I could never deliver that thanks in person to everybody involved.

Steve Melonides and his wife, Elaine, came to visit us again at Wright Patterson. Everybody felt powerless, but Steve was undaunted by the challenge. He came with a juicer, hoping to provide anything that might help move things in a positive direction and some good nutrition to my wasting state. During that visit, and while I was still in the hospital receiving chemotherapy, they visited Becky over at the Fisher House and found her changing Colin's diaper. Steve even made the comment later, "I felt like I could see right through her. She seemed hollow." There was no place for her to hide or reenergize. They both left deeply affected by the scenes and words that played before them like a tragic B movie. This movie was real though!

One touching letter stuck out from that time. It was a note from a C-5 enlisted crewmember that I had flown with a couple of times. He left the military and moved back home to Indiana since I had last seen him. His letter talked about how much he enjoyed flying with me and that he prayed for my health to return. In the scheduling room, all of us were guilty of looking for that perfect mission to take us to some crazy, far- off place that we could tell our grandkids about. We were used to seeing the Middle East, Africa and North America. When trips came up that took us around the world or Australia, we lobbied for the work shamelessly. The letter he wrote said simply and I'm paraphrasing:

There are great trips and great crews, but I'd take the great crews any day, because they make the trips truly memorable. You are one of those crewmembers that made those trips special.

His words hit an internal chord. Due to my laziness, I never wrote him back and lost the letter in the madness of our dynamic world. At some point in this world or the next, I hope he finds out how uplifting that letter was to my heart.

~

A third round was done without much fanfare, except this time we would rescan the tumor to see if we were making progress. My belly felt softer and even flatter, but I was also losing lots of weight. I was so excited to have another CT done, because I was convinced the "red devil" was doing its job. Once this thing had been shrunk down to size, possibilities of entertaining another surgery were inside my head. The visit with Dr. Johnson to get any results was always short and sweet. She didn't make you wait for the meat of the topic. It wasn't smaller! I sat there stunned. I couldn't believe what she was saying to me. "How could that be?" I uttered. She could only guess that the weight loss was the only thing making it appear different. An Air Force doctor brought me to my knees again and I left the clinic as an empty shell.

Becky and I needed to pick up Meredith from a Mom's Day Out program at a local church. I softly cried all the way there. I was afraid to look over and gauge Becky's response. An emotional eruption stood ready to blow and I struggled to hold it back. I just couldn't let Meredith see me like this. When we arrived, I had to gather myself and dry my eyes. All you had to do was take one look at me to know something was very wrong. I was bald, skinny and had beet red eyes from emotions leaking directly from my soul. I remember picking up my beautiful, blonde haired daughter and squeezing her tightly. I was losing her or maybe more correctly, she was losing me, and she didn't even know it.

We made a trip back to Houston to review things. Dr. Plager agreed that the scan hadn't changed and he wanted to ratchet up the treatment even further. I would have run through walls for him. He gave me hope that we still had a chance and I held onto his every word. I headed back to Louisville and Dayton for more chemotherapy. At some point though, we decided that living in the Fisher House fulltime was just too difficult. We would stay there when I was getting treatment, but go back to Louisville between courses, for more space and help from our families. The kids needed room to be themselves, and Becky was worn out from dealing with all the stress, a toddler, a newborn and a husband who was dwindling away. My parents were incredibly generous and offered us everything they had. Their basement was our haven and the backyard a place to relax. I was able to take trips back to Dayton for checkups and labs, but the increasing doses of chemo were now starting to ravage every part of my body. Mouth sores made it difficult even to drink. I found a local pharmacy where a swish and spit solution helped numb the inside of my mouth and treat the problematic thrush. Diarrhea worsened and made the weight loss issue even more troublesome. Trying to choke down even a single can of Ensure became a chore. I could only pray that all this was worth it.

Three more rounds of increasing doses, worsening side effects and another CT. Once again, we were crushed by the words, "no change." I guess if you are looking for a silver lining, it wasn't getting worse, and I never developed an infection. The fistula was a pain to deal with, but had behaved after its eruption. I was still in the game, but clearly mentally frustrated and physically beaten. Houston decided to change course and now wanted to try massive doses of Ifosfamide. It was one of the agents being used in the first six courses of chemo, but there was some evidence that it might help at a higher level if we stopped all the other drugs to reduce the side effect profile. I was backed into a corner and was willing to do whatever they thought was helpful.

~

In the summer of 1995, my mind really was searching for normalcy. Everything that I had, my career in the Air Force, house, physical health and possibly my family was on the verge of being lost. Was it just a matter of time? I wasn't sure, but with two sets of scans that showed stable disease on a vicious chemotherapy regimen, I searched for ideas to put my professional train back on the tracks. I had a wonderful engineering degree from Purdue, one of the top ten programs in the country. So it seemed obvious in my clouded mind, why not consider going back to West Lafayette when this was done and pursue a Master's Degree? To everybody on the outside looking in, I just needed to wait this thing out, but I was desperate to do something productive again. Living from one round of chemo to another was emptying my professional bucket of pride.

Contacted the Aero/Astro program at Purdue, and they were very willing to have me come up and discuss study plans. I traveled up I-65 to tour the department and meet with several faculty members. They were genuine and glad to entertain any thesis project I wanted to tackle. They knew my training and saw my grades. I was one of theirs. The elephant in the room was me though. I was bald and gaunt with a bulging abdomen. I was very open about my health problems with them. After leaving their offices, it finally became obvious to me that this was not the time and place. I had too much healing to do and the future was just too uncertain. Nobody ever tried to talk me out of this radical plan. I think they realized I had to come to the conclusion myself. To move my family my family to another city to chase a degree that would prepare me for jobs well away from Louisville was just not smart. My brain finally wrapped itself around reality and I headed home for another course of hell.

~

Dr. Plager wanted the first round of high dose ifosfamide to be given at MD Anderson. Becky and the kids stayed with me in Texas for that course. They would visit the hospital and bring snacks, dinners, games or anything that sounded appealing. Colin was still too young to walk, so he just crawled around at high speed, working to keep up with the crowd. After eating dinner one night in a landscaped patio area inside the hospital, Meredith and I couldn't resist a game of chase. To anybody walking by the glass-enclosed space, it must have looked like madness. A very skinny bald guy connected by an IV line to a pole with three or four bags of medicine hanging atop and multiple blue, battery powered pumps below. Thousands of dollars of equipment were flying around and almost tipping as a little girl squealed with delight, trying to escape her dad dragging the world behind him. Becky finally asked us to stop and sweat beaded on my forehead from the rare exercise. It probably wasn't in the treatment protocol, but it was a welcome respite from our circumstances.

Upon finishing that course, it was back and forth between Dayton and Louisville. I completed two more rounds chemotherapy. Eight months of incredibly intensive treatment delivered us no closer to a solution, but I was still alive. I was left looking like a holocaust victim and wondering what was next. Dayton really didn't know what to do with me. The ball was clearly in Dr. Plager's court. I just had to hope and pray again that he had more tricks up his sleeve. It was now early fall of 1995, and time to pick ourselves up by the bootstraps and head back to Houston again. We wondered if even God knew what was coming next.

Chapter 10

Into the Unknown

Disappointment was written everywhere when Becky and I met with Dr. Plager. My once athletic 180 pound build was now gone, and I was left with 140 pounds of skin and bones. I had become so accustomed to the look, since it occurred over an eight-month period, that I couldn't comprehend how striking my wasted body now looked. Clothes just hung off my frame. We had given "the beast" the most aggressive chemotherapy regimen I could possibly take and it didn't make a dent. What was next? Was there even an answer for us to find?

Dr. Plager was always pleasant and optimistic for me. I had seen him now on several occasions, and he always promised more options if any protocol failed. Our conversations must have driven him nuts, because I was always asking about the next step and what ifs. I held onto his every word, looking for hidden meanings, positive or negative. He admitted that the previous eight months of chemotherapy used the most studied treatments for sarcomas. Going to another agent would certainly mean using a drug that was either older or had less data to support its chance of success. There is a reason why certain drugs are frontline protocols and others are backups. We understood from this point forward, we were taking educated guesses about what might help me.

I had what is referred to as an orphan disease. There are so few tumors of my type in the world that it is difficult to collect enough patients into a study for a critical evaluation of drugs, which might be effective. To make matters more interesting and pressing, I happened to have one of the largest hemangiopericytomas ever seen and published in the literature. There wasn't much room for us to make mistakes--and we knew it.

Experimental protocols were at the forefront of our discussion now. Dr. Plager gave me the known statistics of older chemotherapy agents we could consider using, but their probability of success was not promising. Coupling that with my emaciated state, I wasn't ready to sign up for another couple of months of nauseated torture. In fact, I was bent on never going through what I had just experienced ever again. My tumor had been aggressively treated, but not touched by all of our efforts.

Novel agents were now being explored around the country, trying to shut down blood vessels feeding tumors. Dr. Judah Folkman of Boston Children's Hospital had come up with the theory that tumors were turning on the blood vessel--making mechanisms the body used to feed tissue, heal or even grow new muscle mass. In the early to mid-70s, he was laughed out of auditoriums when he presented his ideas. Nobody could comprehend how these concepts could work. They were so locked into their paradigms they thought Dr. Folkman was spewing foolishness. He kept up his work, along with others, and for the next two decades fostered his ideas into a few drugs for trials in real patients. Widespread success was still a dream, but people were now clearly paying attention to this crazy pediatric surgeon from New England and to his dream for a whole new branch of drugs to treat cancer. They would be called angiogenesis inhibitors.

Dr. Plager introduced me to Dr. Folkman's ideas, and he had a new study available for vascular tumors that he felt had promise. Unfortunately, it also had NO data to support its effectiveness in my case. We would be making a leap of faith. Inside, I was ready for that chance and driven in that direction by an unexplained force. I can't pinpoint why I was so willing to become a blatant guinea pig, but blocking blood vessels in a vascular tumor appealed to my logically driven, engineer trained brain. I was in.

I spent the rest of the afternoon signing my life away. The side effect profile, although not nearly as long as what I had just experienced, was still significant. I would be taking alpha interferon injections on a daily basis and having routine blood work followed for the foreseeable future. Fatigue and flu-like symptoms were my promised new companions. As it turned out, they weren't lying, and I should have bought up Tylenol stock!

Returning home finally meant we wouldn't have to make the regular trips to Dayton for chemotherapy. We settled into my parent's basement. For two weeks straight, I lived on regular doses of Tylenol or suffered aches and chills. Interferon was making its presence known, but I no longer had mouth sores and a baldhead, and I started to gain weight as my appetite dramatically improved. With regular doses of pills to ward off the flu symptoms, I was tired, but a pretty happy guy. The major question was whether it was working. Well, something was very different. My blood sugar, which had caused this mess to pop like an ugly boil, improved dramatically with the very first dose of interferon. Waking in the middle of the night became a distant memory, and my life was more routine as long as I had regular meals. Stability seemed to slowly leak into our lives for the first time in ten months.

A return trip to Houston did not give us the golden egg, but it did continue to show evidence of a stable disease. Not perfect news, but I could live with my current state. Fatigue was always present, along with the daily dressing changes for the fistula!

Becky now wondered out loud when we could give our family a real home again. I struggled with commitment, because I wasn't sure what stability really meant for my medical condition. Every decision in our world took the chance to place us back on the knife's edge. Nothing, I repeat nothing would be easy for us. Meredith and Colin had bounced around the country on a bizarre trip for the past ten months without any recognition for how unusual our state really was. How long before it started to affect their minds, personalities or future outlook? Becky and I heartily debated the topic until I finally said, "Uncle." We started looking for a house in the Jeffersontown area, which would be affordable, and near our parents. Finances were an obvious stress point in that search, due to my fixed income and physical uncertainty. I was still petrified of the obvious, but understood that we needed a sturdy platform for our family to grow and thrive.

A couple of angels answered the bell to help us find a house we could afford. My friend, Dan Smith, and his brother, Tommy, had real estate licenses. They took our preferences and scrubbed the list of available homes. They made an incredible offer to do their part free by taking their commission off the price of any house we found to make it more affordable. We were dumbfounded. Weeks of looking finally produced a house near a local park and an elementary school. It needed some work, but it fit the bill. My stubbornness reared its ugly head until I finally realized this is what Becky and the kids really needed, and the house was at a price we felt manageable. We closed on the house in November of 1995, and for the first time in almost a year, we had our household goods from Delaware back in our possession and in a house, we could call our own. We took a deep breath and I personally prayed that we weren't kidding ourselves. Colin was now walking and playing with Meredith. They ran through the halls of our new possession with great abandon. We had come home and God had given us at least a little bit of our answer. I then found the bottle of Tylenol to usher away the chills.

Chapter 11

Searching

Life gently settled into a more peaceful routine, and the guillotine was returned to storage for a while as the tumultuous 1995 year ended. We were quite ready for a fresh, new 1996 and hoping answers were somewhere to be found along our torturous path. I found lots of new house projects to pour my time into. Interferon and fatigue persisted, but I could live with their misbehavior if they kept me in the game.

Painting, landscaping, dry walling and electrical work were all well and good, but my professional state of mind was lost in the abyss. I needed to find some focus, to keep intellectually engaged. As I temporally moved further away from the immediate threat of dying, I finally allowed myself the opportunity to entertain the possibility of another career again. I loved being home with my wife and kids, but had to push forward and find a way to be productive.

With my degree in aeronautical and astronautical engineering, job opportunities were nonexistent in the local area unless I was willing to consider a more industrial type engineering job. My beloved flying career was a distant blip on the radar, as I contemplated going back to school at the University of Louisville to study for some sort of Master's degree. After meeting with faculty members in the engineering school, I was intrigued by a Master's in Engineering Management degree. It would combine some concepts of an MBA with an engineering focus. There was terrific interest in the community from various large employers including UPS, GE and Ford to support the thesis work involved. After discovering I could also get funding from the Veterans Administration, I decided to jump in. School was always a comfortable niche for me and having a sense that my professional ship was sailing again, I felt more at ease than I had since being diagnosed with the tumor.

I began the spring semester, looking a bit out of place, sitting in classes with a much younger population of students, but I didn't care. I was still alive and working towards a goal again. My family was thriving in our house. Question marks still filled every corner of my life. God had a plan; I just wasn't sure what it was just yet. However, I hoped to be getting closer to the line of work that could make both of us happy!

Another trip back to Houston, another scan, more blood work and still the same answer-- little to no change. My blood work reflected a diffuse suppression from the interferon, but nothing unexpected. I was stopped in my tracks by one piece of news though. There were 13 vascular tumor patients in the experimental study using interferon. I was the only one in the group whose condition didn't worsen. Stunned silence filled the white, sterile exam room for a moment as the gravity of that news settled like dust floating by a sunny window. Certainly, I was never one to shut up for very long, but this caused me to sit quietly for a moment. It was hard to grasp that I was the only one that benefitted from the novel use of the drug. My blood sugar levels were dramatically more stable, but would the tumor have remained quiet without this drug? Was this the natural course for my disease? All were questions we couldn't answer. I left Texas, once again, a humble person. Uncertain what all this meant, but I was grateful that for the time being, I could continue thinking about the months ahead versus the hours or days.

Nineteen ninety-six had really become a year of regaining our physical, mental and spiritual selves. The kids were blossoming into amazing people. Even when I wanted to kill Meredith for chopping her long blonde hair off at the scalp along with Colin's, I was able to step back and realize the blessings that Becky and I had. Of course, it still broke my heart to walk into her room and see long strands of hair gathered in an untidy pile on her floor. I took another deep breath and reminded myself that it was only hair, and in the grand scheme of things, it just didn't matter. I was still able to embrace their precious little world. Even with their choppy new "dos." Our journey was about to take a wild swerve into madness, though, and catch us completely off guard again.

Chapter 12

Chaos

September of 1996 brought the normal changing of the seasons in Kentucky, and I was now several classes into my engineering management master's coursework. I had some meetings with UPS engineers, trying to firm up a thesis project. Becky and I were always a bit on edge, but otherwise, we had a home and the kids were healthy. Our settled state was kind of like sitting on the edge of a couch, trying to relax, and just waiting for the doorbell to ring, announcing unwanted visitors.

I had been going to the VA hospital in Louisville and having my blood drawn on a weekly basis, because I was still on interferon. It was still a bit much to contemplate that I was the only one in that study that didn't worsen, so I just didn't go there. Once I picked up the results, I found a friend of my mother who could fax the numbers to the sarcoma clinic in Houston for Dr. Plager to review. Labs didn't mean much to me, but I always tried to scan them looking for the highlighted values showing the highs or lows. I had noticed the trend over the previous several weeks that my hemoglobin and white blood cells were slowly dropping. We attributed it to the interferon, which we knew would suppress my counts. It started getting to the point though, that Dr. Plager felt like I needed to reduce the daily interferon injection dose to see if the numbers would stop falling. It didn't bother me, because the fatigue and flu symptoms were getting old; not that I wasn't willing to put up with anything that kept me alive, but the naps in my car between classes and regularly scheduled Tylenol were a drag on my quality of life.

On this particular September day at the VA, the report had more than just numbers on it! At the bottom of the sheet was a highlighted note stating, "auer rods in blast cells, sent to Pathology." I wasn't a doctor, but something about involving a pathologist wasn't good news. My stomach tightened as I asked the secretary where pathology was in the hospital. She told me, and I immediately found the nearest staircase and headed upstairs. I wasn't sure what I would say when I got there, but I needed answers. After emerging from the stairwell, I walked aimlessly, looking for my target. Panic was starting to set in as the neutral tile floors and fluorescent lights whipped by quickly. Pathology isn't exactly a common destination for the average veteran at the hospital, so my journey was convoluted. I found a back door into the department and wandered about looking for anybody. It was almost the end of the business day, so few people were still around. Finally, somebody spotted me and approached. She asked me if she could help. In a quizzical, short of breath attempt to talk, I shoved the lab paper forward and said, "What are auer rods in blast cells?" The pathology staff member took the paper and stated simply, "It looks like this patient has an acute leukemia." Her face and shoulders quickly dropped, realizing her mistake. "Who are you?" she asked. I returned the favor by responding, "That's me." The pallor of my cheeks and saucer-sized eyes told her all she needed to know before the words ever left my mouth. "You need to see your doctor, right away!" she replied. I turned away and tried desperately to find a way out of the hospital without being noticed, while trying not to fall apart in a hallway or stairwell. There could have been a tornado in my path, but I would have walked blindly into it. My world was collapsing again.

I made it to the car and started driving home with the singular thought; I needed to talk with Dr. Plager and now. Usually, you call the clinic and ask him to call you back, but I had to know what to do! I paged him overhead in the clinic building, he answered the phone, and I told him the results. A painful stillness was broken when he finally responded, "You need a bone marrow test immediately." He went on to repeat several times how unusual it was for me to develop leukemia from the therapy given. He was going to notify the leukemia service at Anderson and get back to me. He seemed as stunned as I was, but from 1000 miles away. I continued driving home, and by the time I was on Hurstbourne Lane in my hometown, I had tears streaming down my face. Curse words and pleading flowed rapidly from my mouth in one direction. God.

Arriving home, I don't remember the conversation with Becky, except the gist was we were very much in trouble again. We sat dumbfounded in the family room as the kids played around us, blissfully unaware of a new mess that had just arrived. I needed to gather myself quickly, because Wright Patterson was the best location for me to obtain a bone marrow tap quickly. Dr. Johnson knew my medical issues and my bills would be completely covered in the military facility. Arrangements were made and the next day we headed to Dayton, Ohio.

That two and a half hour drive was among the longest rides of my life. By this time, I had time to look up acute leukemia and found another life-threatening beast lurking inside me. They had to be sharpening up the guillotine again. They knew my case well in the oncology clinic of the hospital at Wright Patterson. Labs were drawn and I met with Dr. Johnson. She explained the need to draw marrow from my hip. Then they could look at the cell types and make a diagnosis. It wasn't a pleasant procedure, but according to her, it wouldn't last more than a couple of minutes. I was mentally, physically and emotionally numb. After I dressed in a gown, we moved to the minor procedure room of the clinic. Lying on my side on top of one of those nondescript tan exam tables, my hip was prepped, a drape was placed and multiple numbing injections made into my iliac crest or upper hip rim. It burned, but what was more disconcerting was the needle tip hitting and probing the bone as she tried to anesthetize the area. That was the easy part! Now a large core needle was pushed through the skin and up against the bone. With pressure and rotating movements, it cut a core sample for the pathologist. Once again, that was the easy part! Finally, another needle was placed in the same area, but this one was searching for liquid marrow. The fun part started when she pulled on the plunger and tried to aspirate fluid. I was urged to breathe as a stabbing pain engulfed my leg with a throbbing, which I had never felt before in my life. The aspirations lasted about ten seconds for each draw, but unfortunately, they didn't produce any marrow. Another needle pass, more pain, another pass, more pain, another pass, more pain, until Dr. Johnson finally relented. She had made eight or nine attempts before telling me that it was not going to happen. They cleaned me up, sent the core sample to pathology, and I dressed before meeting in her office with Becky. The conversation wasn't pleasant, and in her very direct way, she told me that it was likely unsuccessful, because so many leukemic cells were packing the marrow space, they couldn't be drawn out. We would have to wait for the pathology results on the core sample, which she expected in a couple of days. Her opinion was that the massive chemotherapy for the sarcoma had likely caused the leukemia. It certainly is one of the possibilities, but unusual, since I wasn't treated with the typical agents that cause secondary leukemia. The drive home was quiet. We didn't know the name of this monster, but were well aware that it was a fast-acting cancer, with the potential to kill me in a matter of months. After arriving home, we hung on to each other and the kids with firm embraces, after closing the front door. Nobody driving by our house that night could imagine the chaotic world that was crumbling behind our walls, in our quiet, little neighborhood in Kentucky.

Within a day or two, Dr. Johnson called with the results. Liquid marrow is the best way to make this diagnosis, but with that not available, the pathologist was able to roll the core sample on a slide and deduce that I had an acute myelogenous leukemia (AML). It is the most common form of acute leukemia in adults. She stated that she was willing to support me in any way she could with blood products, antibiotics or other medicines, but it was incurable and I had two or three months to live, because it was secondary to previous therapy. I would likely die from an infection or bleeding to death. Straight and to the point-- she was consistent. I thanked her for her help and hung up the phone. It is impossible to convey that kind of news to your spouse other than just to say it. She was ready to jump on an airplane for Houston right then, but I just sat down and wasn't sure I could go through any more traditional treatment.

For several days, we researched AML and looked for solutions. Chemotherapy was the obvious answer, but all options were on the table. Everything from diets, supplements, acupuncture, aromatherapy and anything else somebody could imagine was reviewed. We went so far as to visit an alternative medicine facility in an adjacent county to Louisville. I had lost faith in what medicine could do for me and was willing to try things, which seemed outrageous. I'm not exaggerating. I closed up mentally, while Becky pursued options. I was lost again inside and mad that God had dragged me along this far only to bleed me to death in the end.

Dr. Plager had made an appointment for me to visit the leukemia service at Anderson. He said they were the best in the world and urged me to keep the appointment that was set up in three days on a Monday. I told my parents that I would go to Houston, but was really considering abandoning traditional care. My mom was flabbergasted and my dad quiet. I can only remember their pleas, "Give them a chance and see what they have to say." I was willing to go that far.

We arranged for Becky's parents to watch the kids and prepared to climb on a jet to Houston. I wondered to myself if this would be the last time that I would ever see my kids, this house or step foot again in Kentucky. The night before leaving, I went to our basement and pulled out the photo albums. I cried with each picture of the kids, our adventures and successes, my time with Becky and the rest of a lifetime's journey packed into several thick binders. The most special pictures were removed and placed in a pile. By the time I was done, I had collected almost 80 photos. I walked next door to see our neighbor, Dean Kennedy. He was a gifted professional illustrator and I always enjoyed visiting his downstairs studio when I came home from class to see his latest project. He had won blue ribbons in prestigious competitions in Los Angeles and New York, but I had a very personal piece I wanted him to draw for me. I explained the trouble I was in, that we were leaving in the morning, and I asked if he could do some type of pencil collage drawing from the unorganized pile of memories I placed in his hands. Tears flowed again. With his mouth agape, he told me he would pray for me and put together something special. I left knowing he would, but I wondered if I would live to see it. I crossed back across my driveway in the stillness of the night, with only a distant streetlight to provide a few shadows. My head was down and I needed to start packing.

Chapter 13

The Healer

The following morning came soon enough, and it was incredibly difficult to leave the kids, since we were going into a great unknown again. Deep down inside though, I felt like I would be back quickly, since chemotherapy had little appeal to my current, warped, irrational thought process. With that said, there were desperate hugs exchanged hoping that they would remember me, just in case things unraveled in the coming weeks and months. "God, please don't let my children grow up without a father," was all I could pray.

For our journey, my mom and dad joined Becky and me, as we traveled to Houston to meet Dr. Jorge Cortes. Dr. Plager kept emphasizing how skilled the leukemia service was. I could only hope now that they could create a miracle for a broken down young man with an incurable disease.

The weather in Houston was the typical warm and humid variety. We found a hotel nearby to the medical center and spent several hours sitting by the pool, talking about the "what ifs." My mom was an RN and adamantly pushed for traditional care. LeRoy mostly sat quietly and listened. Becky was willing to entertain anything, but I was the bull in the corral. I was clearly angry at the world and losing faith in God's plan and the medical community, which seemed unable to give me any answers other than brief stability. Of course, I knew that Anderson was full of the best and brightest. My scars and memories clearly tainted my view though of anything conventional medicine was pushing. An experimental protocol was keeping me around so far, and I wondered if that was where I was headed again. The rest of that Sunday afternoon and evening was quiet as each of us pondered the coming day. I've never been on the frontline of a war with bullets whizzing by my head, but I imagine the predawn moments prior to a big attack might feel a tiny bit like this. The uneasiness dominated you physically and mentally. Anxiety filled all the empty spaces in my mind as we waited. The silence of the moment was deafening.

~

September of 1993 saw growing unrest in Somalia, as some fighters, led by Mohamed Farrah Aidid, became the focus of US forces on the ground trying to restore stability to the region. I was flying heavily throughout that part of the world and making many runs from Cairo to Mogadishu. The same aircraft commander I spent my dollar ride with and almost had us shot down in Yemen was running this mission. Fortunately, by this point, I had nine months of experience flying around the area to help keep watch over what was happening. As we approached Mogadishu in late September, I was sitting in the jump seat and talking with controllers on the ground about our arrival. As we approached the field, I decided to look out to see if I could find the field and noticed we were directly over downtown Mogadishu. Visual flight rules were the primary source of navigation in the region. "What the hell are we doing over the city, Bob," I screamed in a not so pleasant tone! His response was, "It was the closest route to the airfield." As I looked down, I noticed the black plumes of smoke coming from rioters in the streets that were burning tires. We then had a loud discussion about being low and slow over a city full of bad guys with guns, and who knows what else. They would love to take pot shots at a $160 million dollar USAF aircraft, with the chance of bringing it down. He finally realized his error, but by this time we had hit the coast and the airfield was in sight as we made our final turn for landing. One week later, Army Rangers were attempting to engage Aidid's men and they launched an attack in central Mogadishu. During the raid, several helicopters were shot down and 18 soldiers killed. I couldn't help but wonder if any of those same rebel fighters had noticed a giant C-5 flying overhead just a week earlier. Several days after the "Black Hawk Down" episode, I flew one of the casualties home to Dover AFB. During that flight, I took personal notice and reflected on the sacrifice made by the person in the lone casket, sitting in the belly of my airplane. It was a sobering flight home

Weeks later, I landed in the war-stricken land again and watched from my cockpit window as the last of the Rangers on the ground walked single file across the tarmac to our jet. It was a beautiful, sunny day. Nothing was pretty, though, about the scene of young, motivated men climbing aboard to go home after many of them had experienced some of the worst fighting our side has seen since Vietnam. We quickly cleaned our aircrew quarters on the flight deck of Time and Newsweek magazines, which littered the tables of the break areas. Several of the Ranger's officers were going to be traveling in that space for the ride to Cairo, Egypt. The current editions had vivid pictures of dead Americans being drug through the streets of Mogadishu. I was embarrassed that my crew didn't have a sense for what these men had experienced, including the loss of many of their friends. We lifted off from that God forsaken place, and I hoped their sacrifice was worth the price.

I can only imagine what combat really feels like, and I don't want to cheapen it with my unknowing words. My health issues just felt like a chronic mini-war with its own psychological and physical terror. It can't match the acute intensity of real combat, and I'm still in awe for what our fighting forces do to keep freedom a fundamental principle of the United States.

~

After a light breakfast Monday morning, all of us headed over to the Clark Clinic building at M.D. Anderson for labs and another bone marrow. My hips ached with excitement! This time, though, I was taken to a special unit at Anderson that did nothing but bone marrow taps. They heard my horror story and promised this experience would be much different. Two technicians prepped me for the procedure. They were jovial and wore smiles that did indeed light up the room. It helped take the edge off the moment, but I knew what was coming. I was turned on my side again and prepped. Needles were passed, anesthesia given and finally it was time for the marrow to be drawn. I braced myself. With two steady pulls, they had their sample and I was done. It wasn't the most comfortable thing I've experienced, but nothing close to the tap done the previous week. They explained when patients are on interferon, it tends to scar down the marrow. Waiting a couple of days after the interferon is stopped is very helpful, along with gentle steady pressure during the aspiration. I was relieved and now upset that my military oncologist didn't know what seemed to be basic information. Doubt now crept into my thoughts about my AML diagnosis.

A few more hours passed before my appointment time in the leukemia/lymphoma clinic had finally arrived. I was called back and vitals taken. All four of us waited in the tiny exam room for Dr. Cortes to arrive. When he did, his warm, compassionate and genuine demeanor struck me. He had a tall task in front of him. I sat in a defensive body position on top of the exam table with my knees up to my chest and a tightly drawn face. It reflected my mood. He went on to introduce himself, with his Hispanic accent and jet black hair, along with his entourage of nurses and fellows. The room was crowded with people and attitude. I was responsible for all the attitude taking up space, but couldn't help feeling that way due to the cards I had been dealt. We reviewed the labs, and he gave me a more refined diagnosis of refractory anemia with excess blasts in transformation (RAEBT). It fell under the category of myelodysplastic syndromes. Most importantly, it typically evolved into a full blown AML in a very short period of time. We had probably found the RAEBT early due to the weekly blood counts being done for the interferon therapy. Several questions begged to be asked, including, "Was this caused by the previous chemotherapy or current interferon? What was the recommended therapy?" My body language and disposition were obviously combative. I tried to be engaged in the conversation, but struggled due to the previous news given at Wright Patterson. I finally blurted out, "I'm not interested in chemotherapy if you're only going to prolong the inevitable. I was told this is incurable and I am going to die. Is that true?" If he didn't realize it when he walked into the room, he obviously knew it now-- he was going to have to talk me off the ledge. I was intent on jumping, unless someone could convince me otherwise. He spent the next 45 minutes talking about real hope and treatments. He was convinced they offered me a chance to beat this diagnosis. Slowly, I unwrapped my arms from my knees and started to dismantle the sturdy barriers I had constructed in my mind. I was intent on protecting myself from disappointment. Instead, I found a man I could believe in and one who promised me the best care available in the world. The bitterness was still present, but it tasted less harsh as I started to believe this dedicated oncologist from Mexico City. There was never a doubt to anyone in that room that I was still in trouble, but he explained I had a real chance at winning. I was not a hopeless case! My mind struggled with the conflicting information. I wanted so badly to believe what he was saying. We needed to start treatment ASAP and cytogenetic testing on the marrow was needed to further define my prognosis. I wasn't sure what that meant, but I was finally willing to let this man put me through another six months of chemotherapy. We left the clinic with guarded smiles.

Trying to digest the day's events was important, because so many other decisions had to be made. What would we do with the kids? Who would stay there with me? Where would we stay? Dr. Cortes' planned induction therapy meant I would have to stay in

Houston for around eight weeks. The four of us sat down and decided my mom would remain with me until I was released. Becky and my dad would fly home to keep the kids in their normal environment and allow my dad to return to work. These were the most logical decisions we could make, but it also meant I might not see the kids again for two months. Dinner that night wasn't a celebration. However, we had a plan and a doctor all of us agreed would give us the best chance to find our way home. Our mood-- or maybe I should say my mood-- had changed as we enjoyed the most relaxed dinner since leukemia became too well known in our world.

Becky and Dad returned home the next day, as my mom and I went to work finding a place to live. A very affordable, simple and convenient motel was within a mile of the medical center. The staff spoke little English. They were good as gold to us and provided a clean place to stay while undergoing treatment.

The following Monday was D-day. That meant starting the high-risk protocol in-house at M.D. Anderson's hospital. Ugly memories were hard to ignore as I prepared to be admitted to the same facility, which saw me lose 30 units of blood just 18 months earlier. Before going into the hospital, I had one last meeting with Dr. Cortes to review labs and other tests again. This time it was just him, Mom and me in the room. He arrived with an almost gleeful aura. My cytogenetics had come back early, and he wanted desperately to show me their results. Genetic testing was coming into its own and could give clues to the real causes of the disease process from its very genesis. Finding the exact chromosome abnormality allowed clinicians to predict much more accurately the success rate and possibly even modify the planned treatment protocol for maximum success. Dr. Cortes was bouncing off the walls, because my tests showed an 8:21 translocation. That meant part of the 8 and 21 chromosomes had exchanged tips in the cells that make my blood cells. Bottom line; that problem had the second highest cure rate in AML patients. Everybody feared that I would have a 5 or 7 chromosome deletion, which meant a less than 10% chance of survival. His happiness was so honest and genuine; I found my smile again, even though I fought to keep an even keel. After all, the treatment planned for me was supposed to be brutal. I had an open fistula and with it an open invitation for infection, along with a body that had recently been ravaged by the sarcoma treatment. We couldn't forget that I still carried another beast within and we still didn't know how it would behave during this six-month course, because interferon had to be stopped. Still more questions than answers, but there was now clearly hope as we stepped into the woods again. Hopefully, the path was well marked and we could navigate our way through.

I was admitted, and that afternoon, chemotherapy was scheduled to be started. Before that could begin, I had to make one stop. I visited the hospital's basement barbershop. "Please take it all off," was my simple request. It was another feeble attempt to maintain some control to what was going to happen to my body, but it made me feel better. I left a bit lighter and certainly more aerodynamic. The past several days had given me some time to regroup emotionally. I was surprisingly ready.

Diana was a real champ during the next 5-6 days of in-house treatment. She brought me whatever food I thought sounded good. No limits on calories, sugar or cholesterol. I promised to be a glutton, as long as my gut would take it. Fortunately, I never suffered any nausea or vomiting. I was placed in a high-risk AML study protocol, mostly due to the circumstances surrounding my diagnosis. The arm of the study I was assigned to required me to also take high doses of a form of vitamin A along with the more traditional leukemia chemotherapy. You would think that after all those pills, I might start seeing through walls, but the opposite was actually occurring. By day four, I noticed my distance vision dropping off. Nobody could explain it and eventually I started asking the team to stop the vitamin A. They relented and my vision returned to its baseline. Besides that little bit of excitement, my week in the hospital was pretty boring. I was actually gaining weight! At the end of course, I was discharged and asked to come back to clinic every three days for labs. They promised my blood counts would be far more suppressed than they were even with the aggressive sarcoma treatment. So far, so good, though. I left the grounds for our nearby hotel to wait out the sequelae with my mom. At this point, it seemed too easy. I knew better, but was nonetheless relieved. On the way home, I was ready to eat again, and Mom was anxious to fatten me up. We drove straight for a delicious nearby Mexican restaurant and I ravaged my plate.

Chapter 14

Faithful Walks

Time finally presented the opportunity to explore issues far more important than just my earthly human healing. I didn't realize it at the time, but my faith begged for more internal discussion than I had been willing to give. You might call it laziness or just a stubbornness to think about God and what it was that I truly believed. There are plenty of earlier statements already made in previous chapters where God is referred to during times of anger, frustration, celebration or prayerful hope. Sadly, I never really allowed myself to think about what my faith really meant. As I stayed in Houston to recover from the induction therapy, this was my 40 days in the desert. A time to reflect. A time to pray. A time to think harder about life than I ever have before. It hurt at times, and I was embarrassed at my lack of answers for some very simple questions.

~

Did anybody get the license plate of the truck that hit me, should have been my theme for the first several days out of the hospital. I ached and was physically exhausted. As well as the hospital stay went for the induction therapy, the next 48 hours were awful. Fortunately, I didn't have anywhere to go and just stayed in bed until I started feeling better. Recovery occurred quickly, and I was anxious to get up and do something. The only problem was my counts were scheduled to plummet over the next week, so it really wasn't a good idea to be in public places when that happened. Until then, my mom and I drove around town, hit restaurants and movies and had time just for us. It was a welcome detour from cancer land. When the labs showed the blood counts dropping, I started receiving transfusions of red blood cells or platelets as needed. That's when the walks began.

Our hotel was in an area being rapidly overrun by the expanding medical center. It was very close to Anderson, but still in a small, modest neighborhood. There were few houses around and many open lots filled mostly with sand, weeds and fire ants. The houses were simple, Spanish-style homes with only a single floor and mostly stucco walls. Some of the yards had a very course type of grass, which was not the typical fescue I knew from Kentucky. Sand drifted across the streets, and little traffic found its way off the main thoroughfares feeding the medical monster just a mile away. These few streets would be my exercise and thinking trail for the next several weeks.

Initially, I began my walks out of boredom, but they grew into much more for me as my bone marrow reacted to its beating at the hands of a different malignancy and following chemotherapy. As I made lap after lap, Becky, Meredith and Colin dominated my thoughts. The few neighbors had to wonder who this skinny, shaved head guy was in their neighborhood, but I never saw them figuratively or physically. On many cool mornings, the cold tears I shed made it difficult to focus on the street ahead. Emotionally, I slowly felt the initial honeymoon energy from being in Houston wane from my body as days slid by without my family there. Mom was my saving grace during those moments. It was always hard to ignore the thoughts that I might not go home alive and ever see their faces again. It didn't seem like I was physically dying, but I now knew full well the risks of living in a world with little ability to protect myself from bacterial, viral or fungal infections. I was also still carrying around a massive vascular mass and a fistula that I packed daily. There were lots of reasons for anybody to be concerned as a leukemia patient, and I had to add a couple of extra risk factors to boot. I was an overachiever in life, why make this any different?

~

Something really special started to occur on those walks. I began to pray. It just wasn't the typical, please help me God, prayers. It became the fifteen-minute prayers of help me understand what faith means, and the what am I here for kind of prayers. At the outset, I did lots of talking and God did the listening. Eventually though, I offered up questions and let him fill my mind with thoughts. This process was not easy. As a child in Kentucky, I had watched many families going through the motions at the local Catholic Church. They seemed to be doing their time for 45 minutes each Sunday, then leaving without another thought about what their Christian faith really meant for them in their daily lives. At this point, my health had been in a very threatened state for over one and a half years, and I needed to discover what I believed fundamentally. My engineering logic struggled to deal with the most simple concept of Christianity; faith! It didn't make sense, and I couldn't understand how God could allow so many bad things to happen in the world when he was all powerful. Why?

I was a good person, committed to using all the talents I had, but here I was battling death again. Why? I wanted to believe so badly. Tears continued to be shed as I walked the tiny neighborhood. Praying started to provide me comfort. I had never really felt that before. I wondered if it was my mind becoming accustomed to this emergency state we were living in, or God reaching into my soul trying to help me understand that I wasn't just walking sandy streets, I was taking a journey into a place I had never reached.

~

Several weeks into the post treatment period, my white blood cell counts were at zero and we waited for them to rebound. This was the most dangerous phase, since I had no immune system to protect me. I asked Dr. Cortes if I needed a mask on my brief trips into the clinic building for doctor's visits and labs. He said I could wear one if it made me more comfortable, but just staying out of public places was the most important thing to do. I didn't want to be stupid, but took his advice and never wore a mask unless I needed to come in to see him. Somehow, I felt protected. Maybe it was me being stupid, but a sense of calm inside was starting to grow as I took my walks.

~

I put one foot in front of another in that quiet neighborhood, as awareness finally reached my frontal lobe about where personal success in life came from. I had always committed myself to excellence for each and every task I was assigned. It became my mantra. That attitude exploded in my middle school years as I enjoyed the extra attention given due to good grades. When I arrived in high school, it became my natural obsession to climb the ladder. I wanted to do something special and different from everybody else. Eventually, I earned an Air Force ROTC scholarship to attend one of the top engineering schools in the country and study Aeronautical and Astronautical engineering. It sounded unique and nobody else really knew what it was all about. It was perfect. I was given the opportunity to work in one of the premier satellite control squadrons controlling the Global Positioning System (GPS) and then attended the Air Force's top undergraduate pilot training program called the Euro NATO Joint Jet Pilot Training Program (ENJJPT). I mention my opportunities in life because they just fed my mentality that I had earned everything on my own. One step after another on those sandy streets was helping me to finally realize that nothing in my life had been done on my own. My parents helped me believe in myself and dream beyond big. Becky and the kids gave me energy when I couldn't find it in myself to move forward. They had given me focus in the storm. Friends picked me up and supported me when I fell, and they shielded me from failure when the ship was going down. Now, God held my hand and walked, listened and talked to me, as I doubted him and myself. He had always been there, but I was blinded by my inattention to his presence or unwillingness to put serious thought into what he would mean in my life. Nothing I had ever achieved in life was solo--I had an army standing with me. I just never saw the hundreds, if not thousands, of people who had touched my life in meaningful ways. I felt embarrassed.

~

Finally, we were closing in on the time when my counts should start to rebound, so Becky and the kids came to visit. I was bouncing off the walls. It had been four weeks since I had last seen them. To this point, I had written letters and made tearful cassette recordings and journal entries, just in case I didn't survive to this point. I wanted to make sure they knew how much I loved them and let them know what I was thinking while away from their tender hugs and those beautiful blue eyes. The kids had energy to burn, so we toured Houston parks, fountains or anything we could find to wear them out. The field next to our small two-story hotel was about an acre in size and was mostly weeds. Plenty of sand and dirt for them to stir things up and they did. Unluckily, Colin also found the Texas state nuisance, fire ants. Digging away while playing in a dust, he found a colony, which was happy to show him why they are nasty. Several dozen covered his trunk before we whisked him away, stripped him to a diaper and sprayed him down. He earned lots of red bumps for his effort. Welcome to Texas, young man! We played, laughed, smiled and held each other in such a tender way while they were there. God had kept me around for at least this moment and finally I was starting to understand a little bit of his unconditional love for me.

Just 48 hours into their stay, my counts were starting to rebound, but then came the fever. Nine previous chemotherapy rounds, and now this leukemia induction before finally the dreaded thermometer came out. Yes, I had one, and I needed to go to the ER. Could it have been a minor bug brought by the kids or just the body's response to finally making normal blood cells again? We couldn't take a chance. I was admitted and given every type of antibiotic and antifungal known to man. At least, it seemed like it to me. My IV pole was full of bags and IV pumps to administer the mess at a controlled rate. Blood cultures were taken and repeated 24 hours later. There was never any evidence of any infection, and I was discharged two days later. False alarm, but once again a reminder this was for real and we couldn't relax. Becky and the kids needed to get back to Louisville and we prayed I would be getting on an airplane with my mom in about two weeks to join them.

Labs were my routine now, and I scoured them each and every time looking for worrisome trends. I had learned a lot about blood counts over the previous weeks, but was blown away by the crazy names given to all these cell types in various stages of maturity. Blast cells are the most immature white cells and are normal in small amounts. They grow up into big boys that are capable of protecting you against pathogens you might encounter in normal living. Too many blasts were a problem, since they would crowd out the other cells that were mature enough to do their jobs. Each report found my eyes laser focused looking for trouble. So far, so good. We waited for all the counts to recover to a certain level, so I could be labeled in remission. Bone marrow taps in the middle of this mess were also normal for my stage of treatment. We continued to change the dressing in the fistula and to avoid crowds. I had my own personal nurse to care for me. Her presence was reassuring and a blessing.

Finally, in late October of 1996, I had a critical appointment with Dr. Cortes. We were praying for the remission word as a major review of my current status was done. I sat nervously in the waiting area, pacing between puzzles, magazines and the aquariums scattered about the large space. Multiple patients seemed aimlessly placed around the room wearing masks, but they were really trying to find a corner away from anyone that might be carrying a life-threatening bug. Time slowed to a crawl before my name was called. We quickly gathered our things and headed back to an exam lane after vitals were taken. I could hear Dr. Cortes in adjacent rooms before he finally arrived. His smile gave me the answer I begged for. You could tell he couldn't wait to say it, "You are in remission!" I'm crying now as I write this, and I cried then when he made his announcement. It was such an honest outpouring of human emotions, which oozed from all our pores. The incurable disease was at bay, and we hugged him without shame. He was a bit taken back physically by our response. A smile filled his entire face as we fidgeted in our chairs from the nervous energy. What a gift! God was guiding us through the minefield, and we had found a man who talked me off the ledge and had given me another chance. A CT scan of the mass showed stable disease. I hadn't bled to death, never developed an infection and my blood sugar was controlled with regular meals. I wondered how many cat's lives I had already used!

This news didn't mean I was cured, because I needed another six months of more moderate chemotherapy to improve my chances of staying in remission. I needed a few last tests before leaving the Houston area, and to be hooked up to a billfold sized IV pump with a small bag of chemotherapy attached for the ride home. Details, details, details! My mom and I bounced out of his office, half-stunned, but giddy at the same time. Standing in front of the elevator, we embraced with tears streaming down our faces. The rest of the day was a blur, except the phone call home to share our news. A wildfire of connections spread across our world that we had so far beaten the odds again and were headed home. Grace filled my soul, and I prayed that somehow, I was worth His love.

One more meeting was scheduled with Dr. Cortes before leaving Houston, but I had something I needed to do. There is a company in Arizona that makes almost all the nametags for flyers in the military. I placed a special order and asked for overnight delivery. When we were going over the details of the next six months of maintenance therapy with Dr. Cortes, I told him I had a gift. I pulled out a specially made nametag in my old squadron's colors, but with his name and flight surgeon's wings on it. In a sense, he had kept me flying in life, and I wanted him to have something unique to remember the moment. His face lit up as he accepted the small but symbolic gift. There was no doubt; he knew how grateful I was for the gift of life he had given me. Months down the road, during one of my regular checkups in Houston, he pulled the blue and red stitched nametag out of his white lab coat pocket. Our lives had crossed in a very unique and special way. Our interaction would not end here, though. He had more things to share.

~

In Louisville, our neighbor, Dean Kennedy, toiled away on a labor of love. He spent several weeks transforming a piece of paper into an amazing visual expression of our lives. During that time, he along with his wife Marilyn wondered aloud if I was doing okay. Our last discussion was at night when I arrived with a handful of photos asking him to draw something. I left his porch, obviously upset, and neither of us knew if I would ever witness his work.

He finally couldn't stand it and decided to come over with Marilyn to deliver his gift to Becky and to find out how I was doing. He gently peeled back the paper covering the pencil drawing taped to a piece of cardboard. The room fell apart. It was beautiful beyond description. Good news travels fast, and Dean finally learned that the news from Houston was fantastic. I really would get to see his gift in the coming days. We knew some amazing people surrounded us, but at times, when you are just trying to survive the day, it was difficult to grasp fully. Becky couldn't bring herself to look at the drawing again until I came home. It was too hard, and the emotions too unbridled to re-experience without me by her side. The drawing sat in a corner, away from prying eyes, waiting for another chance to reveal its story soon enough.

~

That evening, my mom and I had a celebration dinner and reminisced about our many memories of Houston and of my childhood. It was a sweet moment of reflection. During our stay, my mom needed to get a haircut, so she set out to find a hairdresser. Just a couple of miles down the street and next to Rice

University, she found a spot. Upon entering, an elderly gentleman greeted her and took her back to a chair. My mom was convinced he was the host and that the hairdresser would be with her shortly. Was she wrong! When he started draping her, panic set in and she felt trapped. He went on to cut away until little was left. Spinning her chair around for the unveiling left my mom speechless. She just threw money at him and left like the wind. As she walked into our hotel room, she threw her hands in the air and kept saying, "I'm ruined," over and over. I couldn't help chuckling inside, but not so she could see me. I mean, if something like this was ever going to happen, Houston was the perfect location. Nobody knew her. You couldn't convince her, though, and she puffed on her cigarettes outside our door as if she were a woman on death row. At our celebration dinner, I finally got to laugh heartily at that moment, and she relented with a smile of her own. We had survived one mess after another together, and her hair had almost completely recovered from the bob job.

Late that night, after packing and making airline arrangements, I sat outside and enjoyed the warm, moist breeze of this Southern city. I was alone and trying to take in the day's events. I wept openly, frequently and with little restraint on those metal fire escape steps. Maybe I would grow old with my wife and help raise our children. We were proving daily that anything was truly possible. Just barely lit, the sandy streets sat quiet in the distance, but surrounding me. Those walks opened a spiritual journey for me, and in a sense, they still encircle my life.

Chapter 15

Lost

Well-wishers filled our world as my mom and I returned to Louisville. Family and friends called or visited to see the miracle man. Becky was the pillar of my life, though. When things were beyond upside down, I could always find comfort in her arms. We just looked forward to some boring days of taking care of the kids. Before settling in, she had to show me something. Dean's gift had waited patiently in the corner for me to arrive. Becky almost seemed afraid to touch it. There were so many emotions living in that piece through the pictures Dean had majestically woven together in an amazing collage. I picked it up and did my own unveiling to find a piece of Dean's work, which was priceless in our eyes. Emotions filled our little room as we finally allowed ourselves the chance to think about tomorrow again.

I still had the wallet sized pump and tiny IV bag connected to the chest port under my clothes, administering the first of six maintenance doses of chemo. When it completed in three days, I was supposed to place the slick little device in a box for return shipment to Anderson. It was a great system where people outside the local Houston area could receive their care through Anderson, but not have to incur the costs of lodging and meals away from home. Regular labs continued, and I now made contact with Dr. Terry Hadley of the Brown Cancer Center and the University of Louisville. He had agreed to handle my care between visits to see Dr. Cortes. That collaboration made my ongoing treatment much more manageable. He was a wonderful, compassionate man, who became instantly engaged in my case. I loved talking with him, because you could see his focus on everything you had to say. Another angel presented to me front and center.

Every two months, I headed back to Texas for bone marrow taps and extensive lab work. Each time, the news was positive. Professional plans for my future were somehow not out of the question anymore. I still carried the beast, but it was behaving and for the moment, my leukemia was in remission. Coursework for the engineering master's degree, which were dropped mid-semester six months prior, were restarted. My mind needed and wanted normalcy as well. The future was obviously still quite cloudy, but I wanted to get back on the road to being functional. Classes and life regained some momentum as 1997 arrived with another breath of fresh air. I was mentally and physically alive again and looking for professional and personal projects to get my hands dirty. Where would I start?

~

We were so fortunate to have Becky's dad, Pops, in our lives. His big round glasses didn't hide his prominent nose, but his face was dominated every day with a smile that lit up every room. He never met a stranger and he greeted you with the deepest hugs that let you know you were loved from his core. Pops just had a special energy that could pick up a room on his entrance. He was also a gifted cabinetmaker!

In the middle of my treatment and recovery in Houston, I decided to make something unique and special for Becky that would last far longer than I possibly could. She had always talked about having a china cabinet to display beautiful things we had, but were relegated to boxes buried in the deep, dark crevices of our basement. We weren't even sure what we had, since we so rarely went looking for them. I told Becky I wanted to build her a corner china cabinet, since that is what I thought I could handle with Pop's help. I could immediately see the gyros spinning in her head quickly come up to speed with grand ideas. I started to wonder if I was creating my own monster. Her task was to find a design she liked and we would build it. After weeks of looking through furniture books and visiting local stores, she was frustrated and ready to give up. Nothing caught her fancy, until she walked through a final store and found her prize. She took pictures and was even able to obtain a copy of the piece's dimensions and more pictures from the store's catalog. She came home with a little extra hop in her step and a sly grin to announce her successful pilgrimage. I took a look at her prize in the catalog and tried to hold steady when I found a seven foot tall and six foot long behemoth piece. My head was lost in the grandiosity of the gorgeous cabinet as I sheepishly muttered, "Let's see if Pops thinks we can build it." I certainly didn't know where to start. The furniture I planned on tackling had just been placed on steroids and was probably three times the size I originally envisioned.

Pops was always up for a challenge and when he was shown the pictures and dimensions, he quite nonchalantly announced that we could do it. I looked up at him somewhat dumbfounded, but was willing to entertain the possibility. He was going to have to be the brains of the operation and I would be the cheap labor. I knew my role. Days later, we visited his barn and started culling through various types of hardwood that had been cut down 30 years ago for future projects. His brother, Doug, had an excavating business, and when he needed to take out a large tree on a job site, he would call Pops and ask him if he wanted it. Of course, Pops never turned down a chance to obtain free hardwood. He would call a friend with a portable sawmill and make a deal for a 50-50 split of the lumber created. Both came away happy and decades would pass before a project might come up that required the tree to finally display its brilliance once again in somebody's house.

Due to the size of the cabinet and the type of lumber he had available in the almost haphazard stacks, cherry was going to be the choice of wood. I had no idea what I was looking at except to say it looked like boards you would build a barn with. The surface was an ugly deep brown with a coarseness that had protected its interior for decades. We spent hours pulling boards and loading them into the pickup until we had enough to really get the growing project up and running. Pops had been a cabinetmaker for over forty years and had a real gift for tackling any new or refinishing job. He was now in his seventies and had sold his shop to two other cabinetmakers, Brian and Randy. Working part time, he was still the primary cabinetmaker in the shop, though. They took his highly crafted work, sanded it and sprayed a finish on it to make it a work of art. Together, they were true artisans.

Back in the shop, Pops and I drug the endless stack of odd shaped barn wood upstairs to the planer to see what we had.

Feeding pieces in to trim off the rough outer layer revealed a wood that finally was getting its chance to exhibit its beauty for the first time in decades. My mouth opened as we slowly shaved away the rough exterior. Looking at the pictures and dimensions, Pops was so far ahead of me, as he was calculating in his head the length, width and number of pieces to begin assembling the framework. He pursed his lips high on his teeth with each mental process. I simply waited for instructions to start cutting at the table saw. I could handle that. Hours later, we had a pile of cherry wood that would have cost a fortune from a lumberyard, ready to be meticulously cut into various sizes and assembled into the basic framework.

This routine would continue for weeks, as we always needed more of that ugly barn wood to fashion into the solid hardwood base, trim and more trim. I was becoming obsessed with the detail pieces, because they added so much depth to the facade and fine character to the piece, as it grew into something to behold. Drawers were cut and assembled with dovetailed joints until they fit their home just right. The various doors, some square and others tall, required the straightest boards and were meticulously picked with Pop's trained eyes, then fitted using dowel joints to strengthen them. Scattered pieces were now all over the shop, but a vision was coming together. Pops probably was about to go mad working with me, because I was a perfectionist, and he was focused on finishing projects. I helped him keep his sanity by coming in to the shop at odd hours to sand, fill holes, sand, and fill more holes, until I was satisfied it was just right. Pops always just smiled the next morning when he would inspect my work and he kept telling me the boys downstairs could make it perfect with their spray job. I smiled back. He was probably right, but I felt complete inside, knowing it was as perfect as I could make it. My raw fingertips weren't as thrilled over what had just transpired from weeks of endless sanding, but the china cabinet was finally being assembled and wired for lights. Special beveled glass was ordered for the four-foot tall front doors and plate glass and mirrors for various other areas to put that finishing touch in place. It now just needed the magic touch of Brian and Randy to put a beautiful spray job on it to bring it to its full beauty. The final product exceeded all my expectations! I asked several friends to help me take it home for final display. Hours later, it had a home and sat in our humble little abode as a new family treasure. The total cost in materials was several hundred dollars and three months of slaving at odd hours in the shop. Its true value to me, though, was not measurable by what it might cost in a furniture store; it was a priceless gift to my wife and family. Pop's expertise and vision combined with my sore fingers, and Brian and Randy's masterful finishing work had created a piece of art. I could now try to focus again on finding a professional direction.

~

At four and a half years of age, Meredith was now starting to understand our circumstances, but Colin wanted his sissy's attention and playtime. Meredith was more than willing to oblige and drive him around in her Barbie car. Of course, she was the only one in the world allowed to drive the pink and white vehicle.

During early 1997, there were a couple of hiccups with my health. As we were finding out, it was never easy. While changing the dressing in the fistula, something inside the tumor broke loose and crimson fluid rushed out of the opening. It wasn't the volcano eruption, which I experienced at Wright Patterson, but an attention getter nonetheless. Meredith happened to be nearby and became my nurse. I wasn't exactly in a hospital setting. We had to handle it ourselves and quickly. For such a young age, she didn't panic and she found gauze, cotton swabs and saline solution for me. I was lying on my back in bed, just trying to keep my own head. I packed the wound tightly and the bleeding stopped. After years of maintenance, the fistula finally healed, and an untold number of dressing changings thankfully disappeared from our daily routine. It didn't mean we couldn't find other interesting problems.

My blood sugar, magically controlled on interferon, now was steadily raising its ugly head the further I marched away from the heavy-duty induction therapy for the leukemia. One morning, I was confused, unable to get out of bed and hitting my hands together in a strange rhythmic reflex. It took an ambulance ride to the ER again and another dose of D50 to hike my blood sugar back into a normal range.

Eventually, I suffered a car accident on a lonely, twisty road near the house when my blood sugar bottomed again. By God's will, I didn't hurt anyone or anything other than our car. It sent a clear message that something had to change, as complete strangers helped me get home. I'm sure they had to wonder what drugs or alcohol I was taking since my responses didn't make any sense.

After recovering, I called Houston and begged Dr. Plager to put me back on interferon. He consulted Dr. Cortes, and that night, I took my first dose in almost six months. The effect was immediate, as my blood sugar issues disappeared that night like someone had flipped a switch. My relief was tangible. Another dangerous speed bump was navigated and life marched forward.

Inside my head and heart, something was empty, as I continued taking the classes for my master's degree. It was interesting being back in class again, and I was earning A's, but I felt lost. The further I moved into the program, and into developing a thesis project, my mind struggled with the direction I was taking. This was a very unusual feeling that left me quite uneasy. All my life, I seemed to know exactly what I wanted and I would put a laser focus on the target to achieve that goal. Now, I toiled away and questioned whether I was taking the right path. Maybe God made my earlier decisions too easy for me. I now sought out his help and I actively prayed for strength, courage and guidance. Physically, I wasn't strolling the sandy streets of the quiet neighborhood in Houston, but mentally, I relived some of those moments. Prayers for healing and patience turned to requests for direction. I wanted to do something special with the gift of life I had been granted. My current pathway seemed like the wrong use of my skills. I continued taking the classes, as I prayed harder for that guidance. God would respond, but with a very unexpected answer.

In the late spring of 1997, my family and I met my mom and dad for lunch at the local Steak and Shake. It was pretty much a nondescript kind of day. Topics were the typical mundane variety, and of course, included my ongoing maintenance therapy, which was almost completed. I finally dropped the bomb... "What would you think about me going to medical school?" I stated just kind of matter of factly. Faces went blank around the table, and no one seemed ready to offer the first response. Finally, after picking themselves up off the floor, they were in agreement. If that were what I wanted to do, they would stand by me. If any of them had the guts, they should have shot me right there on the spot. The chemo, low blood counts, loss of blood and stress must have cost me any sense I had left. Their only advice was to contact Houston to see what they thought. That seemed reasonable to me, even if I probably had lost my mind.

Within a couple of days, I called Dr. Cortes and discussed the proposition. He never backed down from his initial response. I'm paraphrasing what he said, but it was something like;

Your leukemia is in remission, the mass is currently stable and I don't see why you can't go to medical school.

If there was one person's opinion I valued most about my health status, it was Dr. Cortes. With his encouragement, I stood up and embraced the challenge. I took a deep breath and wondered how to unwind myself from the master's program. However, doubt crowded the back of my busy mind. I felt strangely drawn in this new direction, but I honestly didn't understand the magnitude of the commitment. Whether I was just a fool or guided by the Holy Spirit, I can only say it felt like the latter. My whole life was based on making logical decisions. This was one, I couldn't put my engineering mind around, but it felt right, even as I shook my head with each and every single step. I was finally willing to let God help guide me. It was a faith-filled moment.

The engineering department at the University of Louisville was very understanding. In their eyes, they didn't mind losing a student to the medical school. I finished the semester and visited a different set of counselors for a game plan. Of course, drama had to always be present and this moment was no different.

Shortly thereafter, a letter from the Air Force arrived with a potential-game changing threat. I had been on the temporary retirement list since April 1995. They were basically waiting for me to die, be cured or figure out my level of permanent disability. After three years, they wanted a final decision made on my status. Their notice told me I was going to be removed from the retirement list, lose all my medical benefits and be paid $10,000 dollars severance. Of course, that money would be taken from any VA money that I might be eligible for in their system. I was devastated. Up to this point, my medical insurance had allowed me to seek treatment through Anderson. They had saved my life and kept me around with their specialty care. Air Force doctors were willing to pull the plug on me years ago, and now I was losing the only lifeline I had to the best cancer care in the world. Somehow, they had forgotten I was still carrying around a slowly growing football-sized tumor and was just months out of a high-risk leukemia protocol. Relapse was most likely to occur for me in the first two years. I worked for many amazing people in my eight years of active duty service, yet the medical system wanted me gone. I wasn't ready to go away without a fight. I set up a hearing in San Antonio, Texas at Lackland AFB, to fight like hell for my tether to hope and future care. It was another battle I couldn't lose!

Chapter 16

Battle Royale

As the spring of 1997 wrapped up, a plan of attack for dealing with my impending separation from the USAF was heating up. My brother, Kevin, was skilled in the art of arguing. We spent most of our young lives doing a lot of it while living with each other. When both of us had graduated from college, a sense of love and acceptance found its way into our relationship. I was the type A prototypical first born, and he had been more of the type B relaxed guy with a penchant for fun. Early on, that mixture was somewhat volatile. We finally realized to accept those differences and understand we desperately wanted good things for each other. That turned into an incredible blessing for me, as the hearing in Texas loomed large in the next month or two.

~

Many things happened around me, seemingly driven by God's hand. Kevin becoming an attorney certainly fit that bill. At six foot three, he was the giant of the family. Long and lanky, his stride could be easily noticed from a distance. With his shoulders slightly bent forward and striking his heels at a steep angle, he walked like a happy-go-lucky soul, really belying his professional status. It also showed a bit of his inner self. He was forever young with a very generous heart. In high school, he lost focus and was very fond of being mischievous. That lack of an edge caused his grades to sag and almost cost him a chance to attend the University of Kentucky. Upon arrival in Lexington, there were more things to get into than he could have dreamed. A rough first year resulted. We're not really sure what turned his life around, but after discussions with family members, and I think an honest personal appraisal of his direction, it caused him to realize he was headed nowhere. If he wanted to do something special with his life, he had to change things. He still loved to have fun, but school now had a new level of attention and importance in his life. The last three years of college saw his academic performance skyrocket. The light had come on for this exceptionally bright young man. All of us knew how smart he was--it seemed a real question of desire. Law School drew his interest and in 1991, he was rewarded with admission to the University of Louisville and Kentucky Law Schools. Louisville was about to get somebody that loved to argue crazy points, but with a simple, convincing oratory style, you couldn't resist. He was born for the field.

~

Kevin had been in private practice for several years when my legal quagmire with the Air Force arrived. He never flinched in committing any resources he had to make sure the military heard a case, which showed them the grievous mistake they were contemplating.

All of us understood the magnitude of what was about to be, in a sense, litigated. I was uninsurable with a massive abdominal tumor and only six months out of AML treatment. Everybody receives volumes of junk mail from multiple organizations offering life and disability insurance. For the average 32 year old, the application was simple and coverage obtainable. When you look toward the bottom of those forms, there is always a medical questionnaire with a query about cancer. My forms likely ended up in the circular file cabinet while a chuckle probably slipped out of the person screening the paperwork. Nobody would touch me. Through my medical retirement, I had a moderate life insurance policy, but it was most importantly, the medical insurance, which kept me alive. The Air Force doctors admitted on numerous occasions that they couldn't handle the magnitude of my problems. Losing medical coverage would change the already tenuous game.

Blistering hot summers were a promise in San Antonio, but this one looked to be even more so as Kevin and I arrived. My fraternity brother, Steve, was flying for Delta Air Lines and provided us buddy passes to minimize our costs, but it also required us to fly into Houston. We were on a shoestring budget. A rental car later, and we were on the highway to Lackland AFB. After being yanked out of my flying career in such a violent way, the formality of showing ID to the gate guard seemed foreign, but almost comfortable. It was a clear sign, though, that we were entering a different world and had to play by a completely new set of rules. The Air Force disability board was not there to give out lollipops. They were cleaning house and my case was just another in the stack.

We were as prepared as you could be for having no experience dealing with medical review boards. I had already contacted my senator and representative from Kentucky, asking for their help with my case. Another friend of my parents personally knew a representative from Alaska, who also promised to look into what was transpiring. By the time we had arrived in Texas, multiple Congressional inquiries were started. There could be no doubt in their mind this case would turn into more than just a number. Kevin and I were going to make sure we had their full attention!

The biased process began on a Monday morning where we were introduced to a female Lieutenant Colonel who was assigned by the Air Force to represent me in front of the board. I told her my brother was there to help me, and I was considering letting him do her job. That concept blew her mind, because in her world, he couldn't possibly understand how to do her work effectively, and it would clearly endanger my ability to come out with a successful outcome. Kevin and I remained quiet, but concerned. She went on to review my case with us in her plush, spacious office, filled with memorabilia of past assignments. I couldn't help but notice that her office phone had numerous speed dial buttons on it. They were assigned to the very people on the board who were about to hear my case. Something was very queer about the setup in this system. She then discussed the regulations governing my case. By the time we were leaving her office about an hour later, she had done her best to convince us we had no chance to win and we were playing for chump change. We were incredulous as we sat in her leather seats. The facts were clear, and on reading the regulations, neither Kevin nor I could come to the same conclusions she had during her "presentation." We had some homework to do, so we left, promising to return in two days. Her petite frame, supporting her significant rank and the role she played in this drama, portrayed a sense of accomplishment in beating our expectations down.

As we drove back to the visiting officers' quarters (VOQ), there was no doubt in either of our minds; she was not there for our interests. Her role was a mere formality in ridding the system of dead wood. Military budget cutbacks under President Bill Clinton were in full force, and I was to be shed like a worn out pair of shoes.

The next 48 hours were important for us to get a grasp of the rules of engagement before meeting with her again. We looked up all the regulations personally, and we argued every possible angle the board could consider in reviewing my case. Never did we come up with decisions, which appeared to reflect her review of the regulations. Were we in lala land? After meeting with our assigned attorney again, we presented our points. Because she did nothing all day but prepare service members for the worst, she had become pretty skilled at her art. We left, convinced the worst was coming, even though we felt it was very wrong. Kevin agreed to step aside and let her take the case to the board, because it appeared they wouldn't let him win, no matter what arguments we made. Our logic, although flawed, was that she held all the cards and the system would not let us succeed with an outside attorney. It was a depressing admission on our part. Before I left her office, though, I made sure she knew that I would scream bloody murder to the media about the system and outcome if it were biased and unfair. I promised her that she would see my face on 60 Minutes. She already knew congressional inquiries were in place and needed to be answered. There was profound tension between the two of us.

Boils come to a head when present for a while and especially under warm temperatures. This painful situation was getting ready to explode on the day prior to my hearing. On the Thursday morning prior to my Friday hearing, I sat in the waiting area of my assigned attorney's office. In the room were numerous young airmen who were about to be separated from the Air Force for various reasons. It was impossible not to hear their complaints about the perceived crooked system that was judging them. At least three or four of them were in the corner, speaking loudly in their cluster. I'll never forget what one of them finally said, "If only I had a civilian attorney to represent me here, I might get a fair shake." A message from above had been delivered directly to me through them. My heart raced, and I sat stunned for a minute, before finally going over to them and saying, "Thank you for your advice, good luck today." The dumbfounded appearance on their faces stayed for a moment as they tried to figure out who this guy was thanking them for apparently nothing. The front office person called my name, and I walked away from them with my heart setting a new land speed record. I walked into the Lieutenant Colonel's office and without sitting down, fired her. Thoughts swirled through my mind in rapid succession, but I knew I was making the right decision. She pounced up like a wounded animal and moved rapidly around her desk to tell me I was making a grievous error. Forcefully she said, "You need to call whoever is advising you in the Air Force immediately and talk to them." I simply turned around and walked down the hall, through the waiting area and to the front door. She was hot on my heels screaming, "You are making a huge mistake," over and over again. I finally stopped and said calmly, "At least, if I lose with my brother, I know we gave it our best shot." Quickly, I reached for the door as I turned and disappeared.

The Texas heat hit me in the face as I walked toward the rental car to drive back to the VOQ. Inside, I knew it was right. God had not nudged, but shoved me in the right direction. Now I just had to settle down and try not to speed on an Air Force base filled with cops and speed traps. The adrenaline surge left my hands trembling, but I had to get back to Kevin and start working. We had 24 hours to put together our case!

As I pulled up in front of the simple cinder block two story building, Kevin was relaxing on the balcony of our second floor room in one of those cheap plastic outdoor chairs you buy at Wal-Mart. Leaning back, smoking a cigarette and reading some cheap paperback, he was about to be shocked back into reality. I emerged from the car just below him and yelled, "You're back on the case. I fired her." He jumped up as if he had been shot out of cannon and with an excited tone said, "Let's get to fucking work then." I went upstairs, told him the whole story, and we hugged. It was true; at least with him representing me, the system might not let us win, but we would give my case its just due. We could also set the table for the appeal, which would certainly be following, if my Air Force attorney was right and we lost. One of our greatest fears was that she would not put all the facts out there in the hearing and hurt or destroy my chances during the appeal process.

All the regulations were once again quickly reviewed as we discussed the most applicable rules governing my case. The next twelve hours were a whirlwind of caffeinated drinks, greasy fast food and Kevin writing furiously on his laptop, composing his thoughts. Finally, at midnight, we were looking for a Kinko to print and collate our presentation and handouts. We were in a rare mental zone where you seem to be producing things at a rate faster than physically possible. Since both of us were going to get the chance to present to the board, we practiced our words out loud to ourselves or each other. There wasn't a whole lot of time for critique at this point, but our points needed to be clear and concise. A white box full of papers filled Kevin's arms as we left the copy shop almost two hours later. We were exhausted. Sleeping was going to be a real chore, due to our anxiety and caffeine-induced state. Back in our room, the lights went out, but my mind couldn't stop racing until a couple of hours later when it just gave up.

Several alarms were at the ready and told us it was game time that morning. We dressed in suits and gathered our things. Kevin needed his pretrial smoke, and I certainly wasn't going to stand in his way. The trip over to the hearing was brutally quiet. Both of us had played lots of sports in our day and now it was game time. We sat in the same waiting area where I overheard the airmen discussing their cases. Our assigned time arrived, and we filed into a large rectangular shaped room with multimedia screens and cameras for taping the proceeding. A long table was in front with four distinguished padded chairs across from a smaller table that had only two chairs. We took our seats and the panel was brought into the room. I don't recall the exact makeup, but most if not all the members were Colonels, one of them being a physician. He was not trained in oncology.

The senior panelist introduced the rules and pending action that brought us together. Up to this point, it was all the required fluff and no action. Then came Kevin Jaggers' time. He logically laid out the timeline of my health issues, followed by the care and complications. His presentation was eloquent, but not disrespectful or flippant. Eventually, emotions did leak into his words as he passionately gave a well thought out discussion of the Air Force regulations in play, and the reasons I should receive a retirement, which would allow me to keep my medical insurance. After finishing his last words, he was spent. The board nodded, but as appropriate, gave no indication of their leanings. Now, it was my turn.

I spoke about my career supporting National Defense needs and flying into challenging locations. It was my job and I was willing to give my life for our freedom. Words spilled out in a choppy fashion, as I asked them how they could possibly separate me from my lifeline, when their medical system had failed me. I asked them how they could look at the same rules I reviewed and come up with an answer to pitch me aside. The room was tense with emotion and the weight of a decision, which clearly could mean life or death for me. Questions directed back to me were relatively few. The physician was given my latest CT along with labs, surgical reports and bone marrow testing. I'm not sure how qualified he was to understand the plethora of information we gave him, but we wanted it on record that the board had it available when they made their decision. We couldn't leave any morsel off the table for an appeals court to deny our case on the grounds of a technical error. Kevin was clear and calculating through the past 24 hours.

Leaving the hearing, we were placed in a small room to await their decision. No timeline was given, but we expected to know within a couple of hours. A soda was followed by a hug from my brother. No matter what the result, we had put together an effective argument and could leave Texas proud. Two hours passed before we were called back. Once again, there were rules and fluff before the senior panelist announced their findings. I was given the minimum retirement available to keep my medical insurance. Mission accomplished! Kevin and I embraced and said, "Thank you," through tear-soaked eyes. The panel smiled and exited the room.

Bouncing out into the hallway, we were met by my assigned Air Force attorney. She congratulated us and ushered me quietly into her office to sign the documents. It was a whirlwind of events, sweeping me downstream like a flashflood. She placed papers in front of me and urged me to accept the board's decision. I then saw a look on her face, which caused me to pause. She said, "You need to sign these before someone can review and reject their conclusion or you might lose everything. You also need to call your Representatives and Senators telling them you are very happy with what happened here." My stomach flipped as I realized she was blackmailing me to cover their tracks and keep someone from investigating the most corrupt process I had ever seen in my beloved Air Force. I desperately wanted to tell her I would still tell the world about this mess, but understood it might place my medical benefits in limbo and threaten our future. Biting my tongue, I signed the damn documents and relented.

Kevin was outside the room, still celebrating with the staff, as I emerged from the room. There were brief discussions with some of the panel members before leaving the building. I really was grateful for a result, which could help me continue to see the best oncologists in the world. Inside, the whole mess sickened me and I just wanted to take a bath and get the stink off my skin. We left and hugged again in the hot Texas sun.

It wasn't long before we had checked out of the VOQ and were headed at light speed up the highway to Houston to catch a flight out first thing in the morning. Kevin was always looking for something to get into and the Astros were playing that night in the Astrodome. We had time, nervous energy to burn and we drank the sweetest tasting 20-ounce beers in the world. I'm not sure I saw a single play that night, but I bathed in the magnitude of my brother's greatest gift to me. Our relationship changed during his college years, but that night, I knew I had the most special brother in the world. God was guiding us both in strange, tangled ways. I was truly humbled again by God's presence and my brother's love!

Chapter 17

Setting a New Course

Never a day went by that I couldn't help but think about my own mortality, but it was moving far enough into the rearview mirror for me to consider serious long-term plans. Medical school really was a nutty idea, and it seemed only supported by a desire to do something special with my new, fragile lease on life. I marched down to the University of Louisville counselors' office, needing to see what courses were required for me to apply for the medical school program. The 1997 summer semester was preparing to start, and I didn't want to waste time.

I showed up in the office with a bunch of 18 year olds trying to figure out their lives. Schedules, books, and handouts filled the tables and display cases. I signed in at the front desk to see a person. As misguided as I must have felt at times, my obsessive-compulsive side was showing, as an overworked staff member called me into her office. My needs and direction to her were pretty simple. "I want to go to medical school," I said after shaking her hand. I then showed her my Purdue transcripts and probably expected to hear some glorious announcement from her about how noble it was to be a doctor. Or maybe I expected her to stand in awe of my academic record, as she urged me forward in my search for the Holy Grail. Instead, it was kind of shrug, a deep breath followed by a long-winded explanation on the requirements. Her quick review of my engineering grades was positive, but she noted I had no biology or organic chemistry background. She then produced a list of minimum classes I needed, just to apply. Maybe she hadn't run into many psychotic, post-chemotherapy patients who were driven by God before. I can't imagine why. How many times, maybe even in that day, had students come in stating the same goal? She announced I would need about two years to get ready. I looked her in the eye and said, "I want to apply for the class starting in 1999, so I have nine months." "Can't happen," she said. "Yes, it can. Sign me up for whatever I need and I'll do the work," was my simple response. To her credit, she never blew me off or told me I needed an evaluation with a psychiatrist. Instead, she filled out the paperwork and gave me an honest, stern appraisal of what I was contemplating. She clearly wanted me to understand that organic chemistry is the class where doctor wannabes go before changing majors. It was where the rubber meets the road. She stated, "If you can get through that class, the rest of what you plan is doable." I understood and had heard the same, so I wasn't shocked.

Within a couple of weeks, I was taking several basic biology classes and organic chemistry. Academically, I was always a strong student, especially in chemistry, but here I was trying to remember what a periodic table was 14 years after my last inorganic class at Purdue. My sphincter was wound tight. The first day was memorable because the Chinese instructor stood in front of the class and promised a full syllabus of material, despite the fact the course was being taught in the summer session. Many students like those summer classes, because they are perceived to be easier. I sensed he was worn down by the system of trying to educate students who didn't have his passion for the topic he held dear to his heart. You may not have heard the groan in the room, but you certainly felt it when the professor told everyone of his plan. I didn't expect a cakewalk, so I took it in stride. After class, I went up to him and introduced myself. I made a ballsy request. "I want to go to medical school, and if I do well in your class, will you write me a recommendation letter?" I asked. After sizing me up, he made some remark similar to the following, "If you do the work and warrant the letter, I will write it." Fair enough and I stepped off the stage and back into the mass of students exiting the auditorium.

The next six to eight weeks reactivated brain cells, which hadn't fired in years. There were boatloads of memorization in the biology courses. I had to work very hard to put lists into my rusty brain, which was never my strong suit. Organic, though, after an initial shaking of the neural bushes, fit me like a glove! My mind seemed built for the logic driven reactions and physical reasoning on why things happen. You had to think like an engineer to solve the 3-D molecules and reactions. Voila, I'm an engineer, trained pilot. It was in my wheelhouse. Of course, there also turned out to be a tremendous amount of memorization as well, but the logic stuff kept me engaged and thriving in a course, I worried might be the cemetery for my medicine aspirations. At the end of the semester, I had the top grade in the class. The professor by now knew me personally and he had heard about my medical odyssey. He became a strong advocate for my application and wrote a sparkling recommendation letter that would have helped Benedict

Arnold be admitted. I was grateful as another piece of the puzzle came together.

~

An opportunity for me to give back to the community was provided in 1997. After all the energy so many people had put forth on my behalf, I felt desperate to find a way to help others. I had spent a lot of time throughout my Air Force career doing public speaking, especially giving tours of our GPS satellite control squadron in Colorado Springs. We had a steady flow of high profile people visiting our facilities, including ambassadors, presidents of other countries and high-ranking government or military members. Those experiences honed my skills and gave me a sense of ease in front of crowds.

I hoped to speak to professional groups, schools or churches about making a difference in the world, and that education was a key to success. These were certainly two topics near and dear to my heart. I wrote a letter to the most popular afternoon radio personality in the Louisville metropolitan area on 840 WHAS. I was not sure if I would ever get a response, but two days after mailing the letter, Terry Meiners called my parent's phone in the middle of his show. Initially, I wasn't sure what to say. Honestly, I wondered if my offer for free motivational talks would end up in the trash. He put me on the spot and said, "Are you ready to go on the air?" Swallowing hard, I said, "Sure." Frankly, I probably wasn't, but here was my chance and time to stand up and be counted. It's exactly what I asked for. After waiting on the phone through a couple of segments of his show, he read my letter and introduced me to all his listeners on the 50,000-watt station. My offer was to give free talks to groups in the regional area. The phone rang off the hook for two hours. Days later, people were still calling. Some of them were trying to sell me cancer treatments, others just wanted to talk, but most were very interested in having me present to their group. It's difficult to express how indebted I felt to my community, and this gave me the chance to share a special message focused for each group, and also included love and faith.

One group in particular touched my life, and it turned out to be their simple gift, which brought me to tears. A teacher from Larue County Middle School asked if I would be willing to come down for his class. Larue County is in a rural area about one and a half hours South of Louisville. It is famous for being the birthplace of Abraham Lincoln. I didn't know the exact demographics of the population, but could only imagine that the number of kids earning a college degree was below the state's average. When I arrived on the campus, which had the elementary, middle and high schools sitting in a cluster, I found my way into the office. We were surrounded by the gentle, rolling hills that make Kentucky so beautiful. The teacher arrived to take me to the auditorium. As it turned out, I was speaking to all or most of the middle school. Quickly gathering my military A bag filled with all my flying gear, I tried not to give away my shock at the size of the audience waiting for me behind the approaching double doors. Could I keep a room full of a couple hundred 12 to 15 year olds entertained with my serious message?

The doors opened and all eyes turned to watch me drag my large, canvas bag down the aisle and up to the stage. Chatter quickly became more muffled as I put my things down and collected my thoughts. I was dressed in my Air Force flight suit for full effect. So far so good! As I reached in to grab items from the bag, excitement started to build as gloves, boots, jackets, checklists, and a helmet, among other things, emerged and came into eye's view. I knew I had them. The next 45 minutes went effortlessly. Whether they heard anything I said about school, I'm not sure. I could certainly tell they enjoyed the break from a normal school day. About a dozen students had a special opportunity to wear a piece of the equipment I brought with me. The helmet and mask were the prized elements and the young man picked for the honor, wore a smile across his face as if he had won the lottery. I reveled in the chance to see my audience so entranced. Education was my message for opportunity and success. I prayed before leaving that somebody might find a kernel of motivation from my effort. They were about to turn the tables on me though.

As I put my toys away, a couple of the students approached me on behalf of their classmates and gave me a surprisingly heavy manila envelope. I couldn't help but show my surprise. Never did I ask for or want any gifts. It became obvious, by the character of what I was now holding, it was full of change. The classes had collected pocket money to pay for my drive down to their school. Honestly, I struggled to maintain my composure. Despite my urgings for them to keep the money, they insisted and I finally understood how beautiful the moment and their gesture were. I needed to leave before my emotions became too raw. Closing the car door in the parking lot brought down the house. I had gone there to inspire them, but the gift they gave me let me know how wonderful the people of Kentucky really are.

On reflection of so many of these periods, I finally realized how much I cried. Was I getting old? Was I getting soft or suffering from PTSD? I finally told myself, life was too special not to notice and embrace these special moments, even if it involved exposing emotions held deep down inside for way too long.

~

The next six months were spent toiling away in required classes and a few extras that I hoped would prepare me for the rigors of medical school. It was frustrating having to take sophomore-level biology courses, but the payoff was more advanced coursework like histology. Upper levels classes were mostly filled with pre-med students. I picked their brain for what was coming.

In the meantime, just as I thought I could focus on other parts of my life, my thyroid levels became elevated. I started losing weight, felt anxious, and experienced a resting heart rate over 100 beats per minute. They were classic signs of hyperthyroidism and a simple blood test proved it. Wasting away again, I started to feel like I was on chemotherapy. Eventually, I even lost my wedding ring on campus when it fell off my thin finger. Luckily, for both, we had a fairly easy fix. Two radioablations allowed us to manually control the hormone levels and also helped me with glucose management. I noticed when I was slightly low on thyroid hormone that I didn't burn glucose as quickly. Ahhh, control, and I relished the thought of anything, which gave me some power over my own body. A new, smaller gold wedding band fixed the marital issue.

I met my goal by the end of the spring semester of 1998. The entire post-baccalaureate work was complete, and I just needed to take the MCAT. That test has to be the most comprehensive piece of hell I ever opened. It certainly seemed like all academic disciplines were examined. The physical science, writing and biological science were topics I felt I could survive, but verbal reasoning was my kryptonite. Bizarre passages written in old English just made me nauseous. I finally came to the conclusion that my other sections had to be strong enough to hide my lack of humanities training. The result could not have been more predictable. For being a relatively old man, I did very well in the sciences and writing, but produced a worrisome borderline score in the verbal section. In order to be admitted into a medical school class starting in 1999, it would have to do.

I pressed on and filled out application paperwork for all the medical schools within three hours of Louisville. Fortunately, I was given second applications or inquiries from all of them, but I decided, based on cost, that the University of Louisville and Kentucky were my top priorities. It also minimized how much I would have to disturb my family's stability again. This fact couldn't be overlooked, considering how violent 1995 and 1996 were for us.

Reams of paperwork and interviews became the norm that fall of 1998. I waited anxiously, always wondering if my verbal score, age (33) or health would quietly eliminate me from consideration. One evening at my parents' house, I took the phone call, which changed my professional life. The physician, who was the last to interview me at the University of Kentucky, offered me a spot in their incoming class. The house was rocking that night from the news. Maybe I wasn't crazy. God was either very good or really twisted. Considering I was still alive, it seemed the former had to be the answer.

The following Sunday at mass, I stood up in front of the St Michael Catholic Church congregation and shared my great news. Emotions flowed again, but not just from me. There wasn't a dry eye in the place when they came to their feet because they had supported us through this mad journey. They knew our pain. Over the years, I had lost numerous friends in that church to cancer. I wondered if oncology would be my destination. I couldn't dwell on it long, because the University of Louisville still hadn't made their decision and not having to sell our house would make this challenging training period at least a little more bearable. Our parents and relatives stood ready to help in any way possible. Finally, a letter of acceptance arrived--we wouldn't have to leave town! I was still too stupid to understand what I was signing up for, but I had my wish. The question, however, was it really what I needed?

~

There was a precedent in my life for reaching out over the edge. While living in Colorado Springs, Colorado, as a young lieutenant, I was engaged to Becky and very happy with my life. In the 2d Satellite Control Squadron (2SCS) at Falcon AFB, I had the opportunity to control the Global Positioning System (GPS) while also working for the commander as an executive officer. My future was bright. There was still a small inkling in my heart that still found flying incredibly attractive and sexy. I had always talked about it, but never really acted on those feelings.

One of my dearest fraternity brothers at Purdue was currently in Air Force Undergraduate Pilot Training (UPT) at Columbus, Mississippi. He needed to do a cross-country flight as part of his T-38 training. We talked and found out the weekend he was flying happened to be free for me as well. I traveled up to Buckley Air National Guard Base, just outside of Denver, on a Saturday to meet him. Inside I was buzzing, because Steve was coming into town, but his visit made me mentally revisit the flying issue in greater depth. He was late in arriving, and I strolled around just outside the fence looking at all the F-16s on the ramp. The aeronautical engineer inside me bubbled over. There was energy and excitement on that vast expanse of concrete. Maybe, only I felt it at that instant, but it was there.

Finally, after waiting for almost an hour, a tiny, white dart appeared in the sky and made a pass over the field at 300 knots. Wow! Nice arrival, Steve! A couple of touch and goes finally ended the flight as he rolled up in front of me, with the smell strong smell of JP-4 jet fuel filling the air. After finishing up paperwork, placing pins in the jet and stowing their gear, Steve and his instructor, another Purdue graduate, came over and retrieved the wagging dog at the fence. They gave me the up-close and personal tour of a supersonic trainer. I put on his helmet and sat inside the front cockpit for the mandatory picture. It was a thrilling moment. Inside, my heart had an old feeling, though, and it demanded to be addressed. We spent the next 24 hours drinking beers, talking flying, and our days in West Lafayette together. Steve asked me why I hadn't pursued flying further and I couldn't give him an answer. They left the next day, and our collective heads hurt from the previous night. One thing had changed, though, and I couldn't let it go this time around.

Driving back to Colorado Springs, I spent an hour of intense thought debating whether I should act on this moment. After talking with Becky and my parents, the answer was yes! They had always stood by my side, when I decided to focus on a goal and this one was no different. ENT Federal Credit Union had a branch at Peterson AFB, and that next day, I went inside and asked for a loan officer. I wanted a $3000 loan to earn my private pilot's license through the Aero Club at Peterson. No in-depth questions were asked, and paperwork was drawn up. I signed my life away and headed over to the flight line wanting to start immediately. An old Air Force pilot training instructor and Vietnam War veteran anxiously took me aside and said he could get me ready for military style training if I was ready. I hit the books for ground school that week and started flying shortly thereafter. Over the next six months, I spent my loan money, earned my ground school certificate and private pilot's license. I have to admit, there were some queasy moments learning stalls and spins, but my mind was focused. During testing, I knew every score might mean the end of this dream, so I studied hard to max out the points. I had almost perfect scores in the Air Force Officer Qualification Test (AFOQT) and Federal Aviation Administration (FAA) tests. A friend of mine in the satellite squadron, Captain Terry Richardson, guided me through the process that he had completed just a couple of years earlier. Unfortunately, he didn't graduate, but his advice was invaluable. I followed his application template to a T.

I now needed letters of recommendation to support my dream. Giving so many tours over the years had earned me many kudos from the Wing Commander, Colonel Jimmy Morrell, and I wasn't bashful in asking for his support. He was preparing to leave for another assignment, but he gave me a glowing review before the change of command ceremony. The Vice Wing Commander, Colonel Bob Gravelle, was a much quieter person, but he was an Air Force pilot. I didn't know him well, but I made an appointment to meet him to try to set up a flight in a Cessna, where I could show off my current skills. He agreed, and we headed over to Peterson AFB for a Saturday cruise over the Colorado Springs and the Falcon AFB area. You could tell he had never lost his love for the art of aviation. I asked him to take the yoke about 2/3 the way home, he grinned, did a few steep banked turns and handed the airplane back. No matter what his current job, his demeanor that day told me he considered himself a pilot first with a love for flying that had never left his heart. We landed back at Peterson and taxied in to the Aero Club on another beautiful sunny Colorado day. After finishing the required post flight checklists and paperwork, he shook my hand and said he would have a letter for me shortly. Colonel Gravelle looked like I probably did when Steve flew over my head in that T-38 about six months earlier at Buckley; a kid with shit-eatin' grin on his face that couldn't be wiped off. A week later at Falcon AFB, he called me up to his office to personally hand me his letter. He still wore that same smile. His recommendation was beyond words and it guaranteed the selection committee that there was no surer thing than candidate, Lieutenant Jaggers. I blushed at his comments, sternly shook his hand and possibly said thank you a thousand times. He was thrilled at my response, and he gazed out the window as I left his office, probably lost in some in some far off land as a younger officer flying missions.

The application was now complete and I just had to wait. Since I worked directly for the commander of my squadron, Lieutenant Colonel William Shelton, I wondered if he would be notified before me. Handling the daily duties of the executive officer, I finally took a call, which had my heart racing. It was somebody calling from a selection board. I didn't catch the name, because my mind stopped processing once I heard board, but they wanted Lt Col Shelton. He was in a meeting with a couple of other senior officers in the squadron. I stuck my head in the door and told him somebody was on the line from Peterson about a selection board. He said to patch them through. I did so, and then trained every ounce of my hearing on his office to hear the conversation.

Nothing, I couldn't hear a thing over the steady din of noise from squadron cubicles surrounding us. Finally, I heard an excited, "That's great," from inside his office as he hung up the phone and called me in. I pounced up and hit the door like a sack of potatoes. With a monstrous smile, he told me that the pilot training selection board had met, and I was on the list. I erupted with little self-control and yelled, "Alright!" The entire floor around us went deathly silent, and heads from each and every cubicle popped up like turtle heads to see what the commotion was. People just don't act like that in Air Force units. Well, I just did and the look around Lt Col Shelton's office allowed for a moment of laughter and happiness. Nobody quite expected that kind of a reaction from me in front of our boss. It happened, and he couldn't have been more excited for me. Several officers happened to drop by and offer their congratulations, but before long, another phone call came from the same person at Peterson. I patched them through again and panicked, wondering if they had made a mistake. I was no longer trying to hide my attention to his phone call anymore. He hung up and called me in again. This time, the smile had somehow grown bigger as he announced to the room that I had not only been accepted into Air Force Pilot Training, but was one of five percent of applicants being sent to their elite school at Sheppard AFB for the Euro NATO Joint Jet Pilot Training (ENJJPT) for training to become a fighter pilot. I almost fell on the floor as the pats on my back probably kept me from passing out. Lt Col Shelton looked at me and told me I was going to be worthless the rest of the day, so go home and celebrate with Becky, by then my wife. Running probably wasn't proper protocol in my blues, but I damn near sprinted out to my car and home. The typical bright, sunny Colorado sky almost blinded my drive home, as I tried desperately to reach Becky. She was at work, handling the customer service staff at Current. Everybody I knew in the world had heard within the next hour except for the person I wanted to celebrate with most. I picked up a six-pack of beer and waited for her shift to end. I ran to a local florist, picked up a dozen roses, and sat in her parking lot. When she came out, I walked up, gave her the flowers with a blank look dominating her face. "What's going on?" she said. I blurted out, "We are going to Texas to fly jets, and I'm going to be a fighter pilot." She knew how much this meant to me as we hugged and kissed. The world was spinning freely, and a childhood dream had just come true!

The next morning back in the squadron, I was still emotionally numb as I walked in to my office to find a personal note waiting for me. Lt Col Shelton put a set of Air Force pilot wings on top of my calendar with the inscription, "Now you have a new goal. Congratulations and Best Wishes, Lt Col Shelton." On graduation from ENJJPT in May of 1992, those were the wings pinned on my chest by my best friend and wife, Becky.

Chapter 18
The Long Journey

If I thought the work to get into medical school was challenging, then the coming four years was about to be a very rude awakening. For six months, I waited for the Fall, 1999, medical school year to begin. I elected to do some medical research to keep my mind busy, in addition to maximizing my final chance to be an uninterrupted dad and husband. My annual trip to Houston also occurred as Anderson monitored my AML recovery and the hemangiopericytoma status. We were now over four years into dealing with the beast. Each and every CT scan and review was nerve-wracking but they continued to show little change. A savvy radiology fellow at Anderson decided to go back and look at the original scans and found the mass was growing about 2-3mm per year. The growth was imperceptible from year-to-year, but when you looked at CT's done a couple of years apart, it was clearly there. We could only hope that by the time size became an issue, somebody would come up with a better mousetrap to keep the mass at bay. I never left Houston with a clean bill of health, but Dr. Plager always promised more options for me, if needed. His reassuring demeanor was a great salve for my greatest anxiety: leaving my family behind to pick up the pieces. Until then, interferon and its flu-like symptoms, fatigue and suppressed blood counts would remain my close compatriots. For now, I needed to gather all my strength for an intense period of learning. Drug side effects or not, we were headed on a long journey.

Starting school in August of 1999 was incredibly exciting. White coat ceremonies around the country introduced all the new medical students to the concept of becoming a healer. It was really a symbolic gesture to show our entrance into this respected field. There was a sense of responsibility, which came with wearing that jacket. Patients responded to you differently and expected knowledge and ability from your position. It was intimidating to some degree as we began the transformation into medical students.

The intensity of coursework became apparent in the first week. Volumes of notes and chapters were devoured in the lecture halls, as I struggled to hold onto the train as it whisked through the station. There was never enough time to prepare, review, study or feel comfortable with any lesson. You were perpetually playing catch-up. I found myself surrounded by the best and brightest that most universities or colleges produced. These motivated young men and women all had their own reasons for being there. Admission to medical school might have been an absolute expectation for many, who came from families of multiple doctors, but for others, it was a celebration of a family's success in fostering the belief that anything was possible for their loved one. There were all types of people present, but the work didn't care who you were. Even the most brilliant minds finally found a task, which started to saturate their ability to consume the unending amount of material.

We were assigned to pods, where about 20 students were grouped into rooms with cubicles. Those areas were ours to decorate, hangout, study or do projects on several computers available in the back of each room. It also gave us a smaller community to meet people and hopefully take the edge off the brutal learning curve. Over the first semester, many of us became close friends and studied in groups to manage the workload. I spent more time with those classmates than I did with my own family. At times, it was a terribly difficult price to pay for the desire to become a doctor. Becky and the kids would later comment that they didn't remember seeing me very often during medical school. They were right, and I constantly questioned my motivation and sense of direction.

No early memories of that period would be complete without mentioning gross anatomy. You just can't describe the smell of formaldehyde and view of 30-some tables with students crowded around their specimens doing dissections. It was surreal. I never felt queasy, but going up the stairs with classmates, putting on scrubs and gloves and then opening that door on the third floor always grabbed your attention. The laboratory was about 2000 square feet of space, surrounded on three sides with walls that had windows, which started about chest high. Each examination table was about seven feet long, covered by a stainless steel cover, and when opened, revealed your body now covered in a thin, cream-colored cloth to help keep tissue from drying out between lessons. A dissection book was placed in a metal holder as one student read the instructions, while the others tried to decipher what they were seeing as they worked their way along. Numerous anatomy books were strewn about on the various tables and turned to the body part of the day. At the end of this course, most of those books were discarded, due to the stains and odors earned from endless hours studying the human body in detail that I could have never imagined. God had personally designed a brilliantly, complicated piece of machinery. I only wondered if I could ever remember all the Latin names.

~

Once a week, we had a class where we discussed the "touchy, feely," side of medicine. It was a rare low stress moment where different topics were brought up, which might affect our ability to care for our patients. Whether it was differences in religion, personalities, social values or anything else, we talked about it. Several students never attended, because either they needed the time to study or rest, but maybe for some, it just didn't speak to them. For me, it meant something special, due to my personal experiences in dealing with the good and bad of the medical system that tried to both bury and save me. I wanted to add to the class and after lecture one day, I asked if I could get up and talk about making a difference. The instructor listened patiently over the next half an hour to my story and was willing to give me whatever time I wanted to make my point. I left the auditorium feeling as if I had found a new puppy. Inside, I wanted desperately for my classmates to understand how incredible their opportunity was to care for the wounded body or spirit. That night, I went home and thought for hours about what I might say.

There was another week of slogging away in the trenches of medical school before it was time for me to talk to the class. The instructor gave me the stage and my emotions quickly spilled out as I discussed my journey. Nothing was sacred in the discussion. Physicians that treated me like a piece of meat or tried to send me home to die were hot topics. The compassionate touch given by Dr. Cortes and Dr. Plager to a scared, hopeless young man had touched many hearts. We cried together and hugged shamelessly as it ended almost one hour later. I'll never forget the look on Eric Schweitz's face as tears streamed down his cheeks, and he squeezed me like an orange. The instructor was speechless when we finished and asked for a break to gather herself before reconvening the class again. As we returned, many of them had questions. The issue of my current health was front and center. I always tried to be brutally honest with my responses. They needed to know my future was always in doubt, but for the time being, I was doing okay and that December would be my five-year anniversary of being diagnosed with the mass and the three year anniversary of being declared in remission from my leukemia. I think we left the room together that day a little different from the shared experience. It was at that moment, I knew I was surrounded by a special group of people who would not only go onto become physicians, but more importantly, healers. I had found a home, or maybe more correctly, God had made a home for me with these gifted students. I was grateful to be there.

~

The rest of the first semester was a blur. It was tough to keep track of months, much less days. I couldn't believe the amount of material we covered. Finally, I started to understand how nice it would have been to have undergraduate courses in anatomy, physiology, embryology, pathology and others to warm me up for the rest of the game. Instead, it was kind of like being thrown into a basketball game midway through a quarter and being expected to perform at the highest level. I was envious of all the pre-med majors now. For my dissection group, I was little help, because I was usually just trying to find the correct page in the book, much less the correct artery or nerve in the arm. I was blessed to become dear friends with Brian Krenzel, who loved anatomy and wanted to be an orthopedic surgeon. I happened to look over his shoulder on more than one occasion to find direction. He had a big, fun-loving personality, which I appreciated. My son, Colin, fell in love with him, because Brian was a total kid at heart. He played football at Duke University, but most importantly, he took the time to rough Colin up anytime we had picnics, ballgames or other events where families could meet the people we spent twelve or more hours a day with working and studying. Brian was a great help to me as well, because I was struggling in his favorite subject, anatomy. We quickly became steadfast study partners.

~

As the end of the semester approached, I needed to accomplish some errands before the mad rush of finals. It was very odd for me not to be in class. I rarely missed. On this day, it almost turned into a catastrophe. I spent the morning driving around town, but planned to make the afternoon lectures. Panic was setting in as my classmates had arranged a special event in my honor and so far, I hadn't shown up for the surprise. They went to great trouble planning things, preparing food, and they even invited Becky and the kids. When she arrived before the actual event around noon, everybody wanted to know where I was. She had no idea. Finally, she made a phone call to find me, and I answered my cell phone while walking up the stairs to the building. Becky did a good job of hiding her real intention, but she quickly got off the phone and the class of almost 150 rushed to their positions. I strolled up the staircase to the second floor of the medical school and into bedlam. I was totally confused when Becky came forward with our kids, along with a couple of my classmates. They wanted to celebrate my three-year anniversary of beating leukemia and my five-year struggle with the tumor. I was overwhelmed. Looking down the hall, I only remember seeing bodies, two or three deep on both sides of the long hallway. Hands reaching out as I tried to walk by and saying, "Thank you." I finally put my hands over my face feebly hiding my emotions. I had seen some tremendous highs and lows in my life, but this was a moment that I still struggle to describe. They really had heard my message and I was feeling theirs. Becoming a doctor was truly more than just a journey of book knowledge. It involved caring for the entire person to include the heart and soul. I prayed again that I was worthy to be there.

~

Finals were as intense as Purdue's and they required about two or three more weeks of preparation. Facts and figures filled my head in a never-ending dance of material being shoved down my throat. I started to wonder if I was given a floppy drive at birth and everybody else a 6 GB memory stick. The more I stuffed, the more that came out the other end. Eventually, I was so saturated with material, I just needed to stop studying and start taking exams. After finishing the last final, I went home and collapsed from mental and physical fatigue. The semester's marathon was over, but another even harder one was perched, ready to begin after the New Year. I couldn't care less. For now, I needed a break.

Chapter 19

The Grind and Boards

As I mentioned earlier, there really was no easy way out of earning the knowledge to move on through medical school. Wave after wave of material filled with impossible details had to be processed, understood and placed into memory banks. Hard work was the only answer, and it required a tremendous amount of time to learn and retain. I struggled mightily with all the memorization and resorted to any trick I could find to give me tools and organize the material for easy retrieval in my mind's closet. I came up with acronyms, silly pictures and used stacks of simple note cards in a brute force method of repeated exposure to the same material so I could remember things. The next one and a half years were exhausting.

Instructors always said the first semester was the easiest academically, but still, it was a rude awakening as all of us adapted to this stressful environment. It did serve the purpose of spinning up our gyros, so we could work at a faster pace and learn how to learn more efficiently. Days and weeks slipped by barely noticed by us; while we tackled the same material other medical students around the country were dealing with, as we learned about the most complex piece of machinery ever designed. It would have been an engineer's heaven, except for the memorization. There was real logic to the electrical, chemical, and physical feedback loops, which kept the body in working order and helped constantly repair parts which were damaged. It was awe-inspiring.

During embryology, we went through the process, starting from a fertilized egg to see the transformation of a few cells into an embryo with multiple organ systems. There were details, details, details! When we discussed the development of the eye, I finally remember thinking this has to be God's work. I couldn't imagine any amount of time, which would allow for the evolution of some tissue ever to become the complex, but small organ, which gives us our view of the world. So much fine anatomy jammed into a tiny space to produce high definition images for our brains to process, interpret and act on was too mind-boggling to me for it just to happen by chance.

Now, that doesn't mean I didn't believe in evolution. I saw real evidence of living organisms adapting to their environments through our microbiology class. Scientific research revealed the mechanisms bacteria and viruses used to become resistant to treatment. It was a complicated, but understandable process. Could someone try to make the argument that we just weren't smart enough to understand how the human eye came into its current state? I guess so, but the more we learn, the more questions and deeper we get lost in trying to explain the beauty of human life. It is unique, and the most powerful force in our environment. No other life form has the ability to love, learn, transform and adapt to what it experiences. Truly amazing.

Becky handled the exhausting day-to-day job of handling two inquisitive and growing kids. She was almost a single mother during this time. My energy was sapped by the endless study hours. Each night I came home, I tried to spend an hour with the kids to keep in touch with their world. It really was too little, but it was what I had. Reality struck me deeply during this period. I knew I was headed into a major commitment by going to medical school, but now I was living the world of truth, and there was no end in sight. I prayed for my health and that the sacrifice all of us were making was worth the pain. Hopefully, Becky and the kids could forgive my time away until this all-consuming task finally ended. Until then, Becky toiled away in our beautiful little home, creating a safety blanket of love and security for them as they grew up and started to understand the world around them. The questions from their little minds would start to become more complicated as their awareness grew.

As the second year of school finally ended in May of 2001, the focus shifted to taking our first set of boards. This was our first test to compare our knowledge on a national scale. It would be a measuring stick, which started to place us in a pecking order for specialty training selection at the end our medical school training. We knew it meant a lot, so the stress level never dropped off as the semester ended. Now we had to focus on prepping for an Everest-sized amount of material to improve our chances of becoming the type of doctor we wanted to become at the end of this process. Certain residency training programs are very attractive due to their quality of life, salaries and type of work. Those specialties only tend to accept applicants with the higher scores. Your initial placement in the class was based on grades earned in all the class work and that dreaded first board score.

Everybody had a different strategy on how to handle the task. I just went with the brute force method of six weeks of study with a single day off per week. That meant taking the test in mid-June, which would give me a couple of weeks off before starting the two years of clinically dominated years. It became increasingly difficult to pour yourself into the cubicle of the library, when the flowers were in bloom, the sun warmed the air, and grass turned green again. By the time six weeks had passed, I saw several of my classmates changing their test dates back and forth, trying to catch their brain at the top of its game, or simply panicking and wanting the thing behind them. If I was known for one thing, it was stubbornness for sticking to a plan. My brain was packed as tightly as it would allow, and I needed to finally take the exam before I was losing more than I was gaining with additional work.

Standardized exams like this are given at approved testing sites. I showed up with my plan for the next four hours to include breaks, snacks, etc. Check-in required multiple IDs, placing all your electronic devices in a locker outside the testing area, and a review of the rules inside a room with about 20 low-walled cubicles and computers at each station. One wall was mostly glass where monitors could watch everybody in the room. You were given earplugs to mask extraneous noise created mostly by some people just there for typing tests. It seemed somewhat maddening that I could be taking a test, which would go a long way in determining my medical specialty, while sitting next to somebody pounding on a keyboard to see if they could type 60 words per minute. This wasn't the time to argue my placement in a room, but it was frustrating. The next four hours were intense as my focus was ratcheted up a notch on page after computer page on questions, pictures, and diagrams on every topic from our first two years of training. We were allowed to take breaks between sections, as long as we didn't exceed the total allowed time. I carefully chose times to minimize any chances of becoming hypoglycemic due to my abdominal mass. I walked outside the building and tried to divert my attention to relax, but that was only partially successful. After a final break, I finished the test and left with little on my mind except for some rest, and to become a husband and father again. Weeks later, I found out I had earned a very solid score, which when combined with my first two years of schoolwork opened the door for almost any type of residency training I might want to pursue after finishing school. Considering the odds stacked against us, the trip through the maze I called life seemed impossible and for all practical purposes, it really was.

Chapter 20

The Clinical Years

Now a dramatic change in style of teaching and material smacked us in the face after switching from classrooms to the hospitals and clinics. It is what we desperately wanted, but it was also associated with a radical shift in learning. Professors no longer spent hours lecturing in front of PowerPoint slides. It was hands-on-training with exposure to the human element. That meant seeing the healing process at one moment, then possibly watching someone die an hour later. All extremes were fair or unfair, depending on your point of view. We were no longer technicians or simple students, learning electrolytes' value to heart function. It was the living, breathing person, which would make our profession unique, as we struggled to minimize human suffering.

I had really decided to take this pathway in life with the absolute expectations of becoming an oncologist. That meant I would need to complete three years of internal medicine training after medical school, followed by two or more years of fellowship training in oncology. My first couple of rotations were about to give me complete exposure to the family practice and internal medicine clinics. All of us were almost giddy to see years of schoolwork finally being applied to caring for patients. There was lots of paperwork, vaccines and personal medical reviews before we were turned loose on the community. Interestingly enough, I had never had chicken pox as a child. I took the required vaccine to protect my patients and myself from exposure to the varicella-zoster virus. After several weeks, additional blood work was drawn to see if I had produced an adequate antibody response. I hadn't. My physiology was clearly not normal, and we wondered if that lack of response was due to my daily interferon injections, damaged bone marrow from leukemia or all the chemotherapy exposure. There were no book answers to explain what was going on, but I took a second vaccine to try to ensure patients were safe as well as myself. I never produced the response we hoped for, but after consultation with infectious disease specialists and MD Anderson, it was decided that interferon was protective in and of itself, and I was probably producing a response, but it was muted by the medication. I would probably never produce enough antibodies to pass normal testing levels. Fortunately, everyone was right, because during my entire period of training and into private practice, I was exposed to numerous patients with chickenpox and shingles, but never showed any outward signs of infection. There really was a halo of protection around me.

The first day of my third year was spent in a private practice setting of internal medicine. Dr. Keith Carter was my initial mentor and he was a quiet, gentle soul. His personality was calming. I was nervous and never wanted to hurt somebody. I was wearing my short white coat, but real physicians had the knee length versions. I arrived with a smile and a brand new stethoscope hanging around my neck. My pockets were stuffed with every type of small reference book known to man. I could look up any disease, discuss any infection or decipher any EKG you could give me, if I was given a couple of hours of heads up to look through my pockets to find the answer. Most medical students looked pretty ridiculous and round, when viewed from behind, due to our overfilled jackets. Dr. Carter took me in stride and told me to go to the emergency room and admit a patient. My heart raced and sank at the same time. I had no idea what to do. We didn't learn this in pathophysiology. What would the ER staff say when I arrived with my blank look? A level of panic set in as I walked across the street to the ER bay to find my patient. Who knows what was wrong with them? I don't recall much except being totally lost. Mentally, I was going Mach 5, but physically, I was losing the race to the tortoise. I interviewed the patient and tried to act as if I knew what was going on, but I'm sure everyone sensed my uneasiness. They were probably afraid of me, but I was more afraid of them. Finally, Dr. Carter arrived and quickly wrote up the admission orders, dictated a history and physical and started the very routine process of getting the patient proper care. I was fatigued by my useless mental gymnastics, while also relieved to finally see what I was supposed to be doing. Outside expectations for me were probably very low, but I didn't realize that. That morning was the first step in another long process of learning to become a doctor.

Family practice clinics were up next. With my swollen jacket, I still looked like a packed mule on the trail leading to Machu Pichu, but I was starting to get the hang of things. Many patients probably enjoyed the painfully slow clinic visits with students, because we would talk to them until our attending physicians rushed us out. Many of the patients were indigent and elderly. Some of them came in with made up complaints, just to find the comfort of human interaction and touch. We would become very familiar with that part of the human agony during those two years and beyond. I enjoyed talking with them, but also started to realize I needed to ferret out real problems while managing my time better so I could get through all the patients on the schedule. It was a challenging task and still one that I find difficult to master at times, even a decade later. Human emotions can cloud the decisions you make daily in caring for real people.

What was becoming more apparent as I finished the first two months of clinics was my frustration with the chronic management of medical problems in a primary care setting. They were the critical linchpin of medicine where most problems are handled or possibly referred to specialists. But, the engineer and pilot in me wanted to fix something. Managing blood pressures, potassium levels and cholesterol was absolutely critical in caring for the masses, but I needed a hands-on type application. As a pilot, I was used to taking a mission, making appropriate plans, walking out to the jet, pushing buttons and grabbing the stick or yoke and rolling down the runway. My simple mind wanted immediate feedback to tell me I was doing something to help this patient along. I was barely into my third year, but I was already uncomfortable about spending a career in internal medicine or oncology. The good news; there was still plenty of time for more exposure to many different fields. I became increasingly anxious to see what surgery was all about.

My friend, Eric Schweitz, who had tried to turn me into orange juice after the talk I gave to our class in the first couple of months of school in 1999, always wanted to be an ophthalmologist. He spent months in strange, broken-down lands working on eye-related projects with professors from other schools with the hope it would help him land a coveted spot in the field. I really had no idea what an eye surgeon did, but my interest was piqued. Being able to fix something with earned physical skills seemed eerily similar to my days spent in jets. I dearly loved my flying career. I searched out more people in the ophthalmology department to find out what they did on a daily basis. We were given only limited exposure to several specialties during the medical school clinical training period, and ophthalmology was one of them. You almost had to know that you wanted one of those fields or the opportunity would be gone before you knew it, and picking a residency would involve a smaller number of options.

While I explored all the possibilities I could, several seemed physically out of reach. General surgery was always known for its backbreaking hours and physical exhaustion. Residents were expected to work 36 hour days, when on call, and an ungodly number when they weren't. Rules seeking to make all of our training more humane went into place during my last two years in school. Various departments struggled to adapt, depending on whom you talked to at the time. The old school of thought was you needed to be in the hospital all the time to see as much as possible, especially patients from the acute stages of presentation through the following 24 hours. There was some real validity to the argument, but it also meant physicians-in-training were pushed to the brink of collapse at times. I knew my own body and taking interferon, carrying a football sized tumor and trying to manage blood sugar issues was not compatible with general surgery. I would never hold up over a five-year period of training. Spending several years with the general surgeons was required for orthopedics and ENT as well. They came off the list quickly. Ophthalmology, with its much shorter procedures, highly technical nature and managing our greatest human sense, had great appeal. Until then, I still had lots of other hospitals and clinics to experience.

For all the reasons listed above, general surgery was seen as the great monster. The University of Louisville had a fabulous reputation for training outstanding general surgeons, but they paid a very intense price with blood, sweat and tears. Depending on their persuasion, many students were looking for either the easiest or the most intense two months' worth of exposure they could find. I just wanted to survive and hoped not to have any blood sugar episodes along the way, which might cause my house of cards to collapse. I spent my two months of surgery at Jewish Hospital and Kosair Children's Hospital in downtown Louisville. Both experiences were quite unique, filled with fascinating thoracic cases from Jewish or pediatric trauma and more routine kids' surgeries at Kosair Children's. I shoved graham crackers down my throat before every case, trying to make sure I never had to excuse myself from the operating room. Fortunately, I never did, even on a lung cancer case, which took almost six hours. It was a challenging two-month period, but I learned how much I loved using my hands again. Primarily, I was just a 5'11" retractor on most cases, but I was able to get my hands dirty and finally see a field where I could directly intervene. My simple mind once again seemed most excited when it could look back on a day's work and see the fruits of all that labor. I needed a career with dexterity as a cornerstone, and eye surgery was becoming more and more appealing.

As the fourth year of school began, I worked out two months of electives, where I could work in the department of ophthalmology under Dr. Hank Kaplan. He was a brilliant man and he was gracious enough to offer me the opportunity to see his world up-close and personal, and I understood how competitive those slots were for residency. I committed any extra time, even weekends, to see surgeries or patients in the clinic. The majority of time, I didn't know the details of what was going on, but I worked hard to pick up as many skills as I could. I also gave a 45-minute talk on Retinopathy of Prematurity to give them a sense I was totally engaged and starting to understand some parts of the diverse field. At the end of my electives, I asked Dr. Kaplan and Dr. Barr, a gifted retina surgeon, if they would consider writing me a letter. Both agreed, and their support was instrumental in the coming months of applications and interviews.

School continued at its usual torrid pace, with departmental tests, quizzes and the highly interactive clinical or hospital approach of always being quizzed in front of your fellow students. A chronic level of stress was always present. I managed to stay up all night when on call, deliver babies, handle heart attacks, suture up faces and deal with child abuse. At times, it was heartbreaking and at others, exhilarating. No doubt, it was human drama in your face on a daily basis.

Some classmates seemed to shrink from the pressure, while others thrived in the intense environment. I watched my study partner and friend, Brian Krenzel, swim in the clinical minefield as if he was born for it. Rounding on patients might start at 4:30 or 5 am. You looked up the morning's labs and imaging studies, then quickly proceeded to examine your patients. Notes had to be placed on every chart. A senior resident was also briefed on your findings, and finally the group under that resident would meet with the assigned attending around 7:30 am. Presentations were done in an almost military style, with very basic demographics, reasons for admission, current status, and a care plan given quickly. You had to be prepared for a simple nod of approval or a flurry of questions thrown at you, which should be clinically relevant to your patient. Done correctly, it was beautiful to watch, but if you weren't prepared, the bloodshed could be vicious. The further you sank, the more rapid the beat down by some attendings. You never wanted to be in the crosshairs. Brian simply got it, so he was able to earn an orthopedic slot at Duke University from his outstanding clinical performance.

The process of placing medical students in residency training programs around the country was incredibly complicated. Based on your board scores, interest and overall class rank, you tried to pick one specialty or two and applied to locations where you could receive that training. There was always a sense of cat and mouse being played by both sides as everybody wants the best program, and every program wants the best incoming residents. Something had to give. You had to be smart and understand what was realistic, or you might find yourself without a match at the end of the game. Applications were followed by interviews and then ranking lists. Programs and students both had a chance to turn in their order of preference to a computer program, running an algorithm to place as many high picks together as possible. The computer solution was legally binding. Around 80% of students were happy or okay with their match, but at least 10% were always visibly dismayed by the result. The announcement is made en masse to the entire class in a special March ceremony of your graduating year.

A few specialties did their matching process early, and ophthalmology was one of them. It was nice to find out early, but it also put serious urgency in making decisions early in your fourth year of school. A central application process allowed us to fill out a single application. All the information was then farmed out to all the programs you wanted to consider your request for training. Of course, there was an application cost, and the more programs you were interested in, the greater the financial pain. I had decided on around ten programs based off quality, reputation, distance from Louisville and cost of living. I couldn't financially handle living in a major metropolitan area with a wife and two small kids. We had to think about elementary and middle schools, thus our assessment was a bit more unique than the average applicants, especially considering I was going to be 38 years old.

Almost every program I sent my paperwork to asked me to come for an interview. There were many dates, which overlapped, but I ended up traveling to seven. Becky went with me to the places I felt especially drawn to, because I needed her opinion on the area. For six weeks, I drove my car from Iowa to Florida, searching for the perfect match. In the beginning, it was fresh and exciting. There was no way you could forget the details and names, right? After a couple of visits, they became a blur. You had an overall sense of whether you felt compatible somewhere, but otherwise, notes, if you made them, became invaluable. Just after New Year's Day, I turned in my list and waited. Louisville was my favorite. I knew I would receive great training and good surgical volume to become a solid ophthalmologist. There were no secrets to what I was getting and it was in my own backyard. We were willing to move, but considering the upheaval we had already experienced, this was a logical, comfortable decision.

Several weeks passed, as we waited for the match results, but school did not let up. Rounds, briefings and presentations were routine by now, but it still presented the same chronic level of stress to keep your attention. The next set of boards had to be taken as well. Same routine in the testing center, but there was not a period of uninterrupted studying available prior to taking the exam.

Match day arrived and everybody anxiously awaited the phone call from your matched program or the School of Medicine. Just before eight AM, I was told I had matched at Louisville. We were thrilled at our fortune. We weren't done yet with training, but it seemed almost fairytale in nature as we looked back on such an unlikely path. I learned to think about things being guided in a God-like manner. I couldn't imagine any human force allowing my family and me to be where we were without special guidance. I simply wasn't supposed to be alive, much less finishing medical school and on my way to become an eye surgeon.

~

My parents were good as gold to us and gave us whatever they had to support this journey. They wanted to take all of us out on a special dinner in Bardstown, Kentucky to celebrate the big news. We dressed up a bit and headed one hour South of Louisville to a quaint little restaurant next to My Old Kentucky Home State Park. Dinner was fabulous, but it couldn't match our sky-high mood. Staying in Louisville was going to be a real blessing and possibly even help us find work afterwards in the local area. Everybody just had a sense of real contentment. On leaving the restaurant that night, we walked to our van for the drive home. My dad was adamant about driving home for some reason. He said he knew the area very well. We agreed and gave him the keys. The van was parked in a small lot with its nose pointed up a fairly steep grade. Everybody settled in and seatbelts were placed as my dad turned the key. He placed it into reverse, but the car didn't move. All of us fidgeted a bit until Becky said, "I set the parking brake down on the left hand side, near your left leg, because of the hill. You just need to release it." LeRoy struggled to find the release lever; he exited the car, turned on the dome light and found it. What happened next was rapid and ugly. He had left the car in reverse. With the car on that hill, when he released the brake, it took off quickly. My dad was struggling to get out of the way, but the driver's side door was pinned against the adjacent car and it shoved him backwards, with the van rapidly gaining speed as it ran down the hill in reverse. He attempted to turn the wheel, hoping it might give him a chance to jump in, but it only made things worse as the front end now moved towards him and overtook his position. He disappeared from sight. I was strapped into the passenger seat and couldn't get free fast enough to help him. Everybody in the back was strictly a passenger at that moment. Fear gripped our every thought.

It couldn't have taken two seconds for the van to rake across the side of a car to our left and it finally came to a stop when it hit two more cars parked behind us, on the other side of the parking lot. I jumped out; honestly wondering if I would find my dad cut in two or crushed by one of the many collisions. Crying could be heard from the back seats. Rushing to the other side of the vehicle, I found him partially underneath with the left front tire on his foot. No blood, no guts, just a flattened foot. I moved the van a couple of feet forward to free him and our hearts began to beat again. We were still in shock as an ambulance and police arrived. Fortunately, there were no major injuries, just some bruised pride for not putting the transmission back in park before getting out of the van. Mike Dahlem was always ready to help and came to Bardstown to give us a lift from the hospital back home. My parents won't even drive through that beautiful little town ever again due to the emotional trauma levied by that event. It was a beautiful celebration, which almost ended in complete tragedy.

~

The end of medical school culminated with the realization of an impossible dream. Taking this route in life was clearly questionable. It simply didn't make any sense. My health was and will always be in question, and if I only had so much time left on this earth, I should have spent every waking moment just being home for my family. There was something driving me in this direction, though. Maybe it is the easy way out to say it was God's will, because I just didn't make irrational decisions. It went against every grain in my body. For some reason, we took Robert Frost's road less traveled, based on guidance that only makes sense to me if it came from heaven.

Pomp and circumstance filled the air on graduation day in May of 2003, but it wasn't the only thing. Our family again gathered as a unit to hold each other. Smiles were broad, but joyful tears found their way into the moment. I sat a couple of rows back from the stage with my classmates, almost in disbelief that this part of the ride was over. As my row stood and we approached the stage, emotions filled my head and chest. I walked up the few steps when my name was called, and the floodgates opened. I couldn't hold it back anymore as drapes were placed around my neck. My chest heaved and I sobbed. Standing in front of the group that walked with me for the past four years, I finally pointed to the sky before leaving center stage and said, "Thank you." No thunderous claps from the clear blue sky were needed. My ability to accept the medical school diploma and the love of my dear family was all I needed to know that God dearly loved me. I sat back down and wiped my face over and over again with tissues offered from my classmates. A wad of moist paper soon filled my hand. We had made it.

Chapter 21

Heaven and Hell

Days finally began to settle into a quiet routine after medical school activities disappeared into the rearview mirror, but we were bubbling with excitement preparing to leave for Hawaii. The past four years had demanded so much time, effort and focus, it was time to take a trip and enjoy each other. Meredith was ready to enter Jefferson County Traditional Middle School and Colin happily plugged along at Wheeler Elementary School. In a sense, we wanted some boring days to unwind. Life had been on a wicked pace for us that didn't seem to relent until now.

The kids couldn't really remember ever being on an airplane. Almost beyond us was the anticipation to see one of the most beautiful places in the world and to do it together without threat of interruption. A state of emergency, either self-inflicted or forced upon us, had ruled our lives for so long, we now looked forward to some sense of normalcy. This was the first step in that process, even though my residency was set to start in July of 2003. We rushed to the airport to get started.

Flying through Los Angeles and finally on to Honolulu, Hawaii was a laborious ride. It was hard to sit still for that long when you weren't allowed to do so for years. I felt like a toddler. Excitement was the drug, which kept us ready for the end result. As we landed and exited the airplane, the sweet smell of fresh flowers, and the embracing gentle ocean breeze announced we had entered heaven. The air came out of my stress balloon. Finding our rental car, we drove down to Waikiki Beach to find our hotel, which had first class accommodations and only accepted military families. It also provided significant discounted rates over the local economy. Eighty-degree weather every day with abundant sunshine gave our souls a bath in luxury. The kids rushed out into the surf and were lost in the endless supply of waves. At night, we walked the beaches to local restaurants and shops, but mostly just to hold hands and be close. Nondescript days escaped us on purpose, but we did visit Diamond Head and toured a rain forest with a fascinating guide. He showed us rarely seen areas of the island including Banyan trees, Bamboo forests, waterfalls, native flowers and birds. That four-hour walk gave us a glimpse of paradise from the inside out. Hanauma Bay was a special treat for us to snorkel and see marine life you could only imagine from watching Discovery Channel shows. The Bay had formed inside a collapsed old volcano and its still waters made it easy for families to enjoy the kaleidoscope of colors swimming by you. It almost seemed like an aquarium due to the variety of living creatures you found. Our kid's fun meter was pegged, but not any higher than ours.

Before leaving that side of Oahu, we visited Pearl Harbor to pay our respects to the sailors, airmen, soldiers and civilians who lost their lives on that fateful day. Another gorgeous day framed the simple, white USS Arizona Memorial along with the constant oil slick present over the wreckage. Becky's father had served on a destroyer as the war ended, along with one of her uncles. The day reminded us of how fortunate we were due to their sacrifices. It also reminded us how fragile life is. As if, we needed to be told again.

We had made arrangements to go over to the opposite side of the island and stay in beachfront housing at Bellows Air Force Station. The military still controlled various pieces of prime real estate in Hawaii due to the services significant presence since World War II. The islands continue to serve as a major gateway to the Pacific. Bellows was a leftover piece of Heaven that used to have an airstrip. Multiple small buildings were scattered about the stunning coastline, and military members could rent duplexes on the beach for almost nothing. Demand was high, so three days was your maximum stay. There was nothing fancy about the cinder block buildings hidden amongst the impossibly tilted palm trees and simple crushed shell/sand driveways. Inside were two bedrooms, tile floors, a small TV area, but the coup de gras was outside the sliding glass door. Only ten paces were needed to stand in the aqua blue waters of the Pacific Ocean. Hawaii's rugged mountains were perched several miles away and were covered with dense green vegetation that made you think of Elvis Presley movies. The waves on this side were more aggressive, but a welcome challenge for my body board and me. For three days, we grilled out in the backyard next to the full glory of paradise. Life slowed to a crawl. To have it ever end was a bit depressing, but we had seen, experienced and tasted the good life again. We headed back to the airport to catch our flight, but not before buying a few leis to take a bit of the island home with us to Kentucky.

Several weeks remained before I began training for my new profession. We focused inwardly and spent the majority of that time forging our family relationships. Becky had carried the burden almost exclusively for over four years, but I always wanted to be a father the kids could rely on, come to and love for a lifetime as they transformed into adults. These were small steps, but I was desperate for Becky, Meredith and Colin to know how much I loved them. Their presence in my life had already helped lift me through impossible tangled messes. It wasn't about to get any easier for us.

As my 38th Birthday approached at the end of June, I was trying to ready myself mentally and physically for the onslaught of residency. Something very concerning happened. Having a football-sized tumor sitting in your abdomen not only created a very noticeable bulge, but also shoved all the major organs to the side, almost like a pregnancy might. It was amazing that I never had any bowel obstructions or pain. I had dealt with chronic diarrhea for years. As July 1st approached, an ominous sign moved front and center when I developed black stools. The smell was unmistakable. I had a GI bleed. Initially, I tried to stick my head in the sand and ignore the symptoms. Half a day passed and I was still bleeding. I couldn't ignore it any longer and told Becky I needed to go to the ER for labs and possibly a scope. She was dumbfounded. I was a doctor now, I had to know what was going on, she thought. Calling my primary care doctor, Dr. Bill French, he asked a GI person to come and evaluate me in the ER. Labs reflected my loss of blood as my hemoglobin drifted down into the

9-10 range (normal adult male range is 14-16). I was used to living with a hemoglobin level around 12 due to the effects of the interferon. An upper GI endoscopy was performed, but didn't find any ulcers or tumors, which might be causing the problem. A reflection of my past and present medical issues finally pointed to the likely culprit, portal hypertension. It is typically associated with liver disease, but in my case, the abdominal tumor was dumping so much blood into the drainage system that courses through the liver, the portal venous system, high pressures resulted and were causing the blood to back up into my GI tract. Would it stop? Would this become a chronic issue? Was I going to bleed to death? None of those questions had straightforward answers. I was admitted to the hospital for observation and a possible transfusion, if needed.

Again, I was being pushed to the edge and wondering if this is how it all unravels. I was angry at the fact I worked so hard to get through school and just as I'm about to start specialty training, it all looked so precarious. What did God want from me? I sat quietly in the hospital room, hoping a relaxed state would stop the bleeding before a transfusion became necessary. Meredith spent the night with me. At ten years of age, she was no longer the naive little toddler with no idea what was happening. Concern easily found its way to her cherubic face. Inside, all of us were a mess again.

Forty-eight hours later, the bleed stopped and we collectively sighed. This was a new problem with fresh issues to manage. I started taking a beta blocker, which was proven through studies to minimize GI bleeds in patients with portal hypertension. We prayed that it worked and asked for guidance. Should I throw away my ophthalmology training slot or press forward? Nobody had the magical answer and gut feelings again led me to believe I needed to continue with the present plan. Several days later, I began my first day of an internal medicine year, which was required for all incoming ophthalmology residents before the eye training began in earnest.

My health continued to present bizarre challenges in care, management and planning for a future life. Maybe I was too stubborn to quit or know when I was ahead. I constantly had to evaluate whether my health could possibly jeopardize patient care. I was desperate to make a difference in people's lives as a physician and hurting someone would have destroyed me emotionally. So far, the answer I came up with was always the same; no. Something inside kept telling me I was on the right course, hang on and deal with the changes. My mission was still set in my mind, but worries and reality again fogged my course.

Chapter 22

The Wait

A piece of advice for everybody, avoid a major trauma hospital on every July 1st, if at all possible. That is the annual date when the just graduated medical students show up as interns for the various programs, and residents assume the next role up the chain. You will still receive proper care, but extended wait times and blank looks are likely to be routine for at least the next 6-8 weeks. A very quick maturation process rolls across all medical campuses like a wrecking ball. It is a painful process. Everybody is adjusting to their new roles, either as new doctors or senior residents.

I showed up in the ophthalmology department for a month long elective, but I was really assigned to the internal medicine department for the following year. It was part of the overall exposure to medicine, prepping us for the following three years of eye training and surgery. I felt some anxiety in this elective month, because I was trying to be useful in the clinics even though I had few skills to help me do the thorough exam required of an ophthalmologist. You never want to embarrass yourself in front of your new employer, even if you were merely window dressing to them right now. The new issue of GI bleeds was fresh in my mind as well. Fortunately, I wasn't currently bleeding, but my blood counts were down. I was standing closer to a fragile cliff, tired, but still capable.

I was determined to pick as many skills from the ophthalmology residents as possible. Maybe I would retain some nuggets for later when the burden fell squarely on my shoulders. It was a brief month. In the end, I reluctantly left the eye service for the medicine clinics and hospital wards. As a medical intern, I had senior residents above me to oversee my work, but I was the first physician to see a patient in the clinic or emergency room. There was always that backup. However, it just felt different now since you had MD next to your name. There were always tons of questions. My pockets remained ridiculously full of all those books to help me in acute situations. Every variety of medical problems was seen during that year. A sense of seasoning was occurring for all of us, due to the volume of work and exposure. Within a couple of months, we handled most of what came across our plates without batting an eye. I once again realized how much I wanted to be in a surgical field, but I also came to appreciate how important the various services were in taking care of all a patient's needs. Training doctors ordered too many tests and sent patients for studies, which probably didn't help in the analysis of their conditions. It was an accepted byproduct of learning our trade. Maturation brought with it smarter decisions and less money spent. Time was a real friend to us, because it brought experience.

The cardiac intensive care unit gave me my own level of heart stress. It was the hardest month of the year. About four doctors were assigned each month to handle patients needing evaluation by the cardiologists in the hospital. We were called when a cardiology consult or related urgent problem was encountered. EKGs were part of our training, but they were now attached to a patient who might be dying. A fellow was always available to us 24 hours a day. Time was critical, since heart tissue might be dying throughout any evaluation. We had to make quick decisions, so it was quite stressful. When you were on call, consults were called in for floor or ER patients constantly. It was a never-ending revolving door of work. If you combine that, with staying in the hospital for 36 hours every couple of days, fatigue slows your thought processes. My cardiology fellow was awesome, and I used him frequently throughout the month. Fortunately, I survived the heart world without maiming someone. My constant prayer each day was for guidance and knowledge to help and never to hurt the people in my care. I thanked God at the end of the month for deliverance to a new clinic.

My internship ended in June of 2004 and my health never managed to become a major issue. I was still making the annual visits to Houston. They continued to reveal a huge abdominal mass that was growing very slowly, but not invading any of the surrounding tissue. My blood counts were now lower than previous visits, but that was now due to the brief, periodic bleeds. Thankfully, there was still no evidence of leukemia. My bone marrow worked overtime to keep up with my body's needs and the result was more chronic fatigue. I had been dealing with it for so long now, it just seemed part of my day. Whenever possible, I would take naps to help keep my body from failing me. It was a brutal dance, but I had made the choice of this career. Adaption would have to be a key skill if I was going to survive the coming years.

Chapter 23

Exhaustion

"To whom much has been given, much is expected in return."

Luke 12:48

~

Years of training and studying were now allowing a dream to come to fruition in July of 2004. Ophthalmology training was ready to dominate the time clock as nothing else ever had in my life. It was what I asked for, but was it what I expected? The coming months were about to introduce my scarred body to the cruel reality of training to become an eye surgeon. Most of the other specialties would chuckle about our perceived soft lifestyle, but they had no idea what our work was all about. Private practice might be a different story, but ophthalmology residents worked very hard and fielded calls at all hours of the night. Sleep was about to become my distant cousin whom I rarely visited.

Day one began with introductions and training sessions on how to complete exams, use equipment, fill out paperwork and find help if you needed it. We had a unique language to describe our findings. Few doctors knew how to read our charts, but I think we almost liked it better that way. Our world was foreign and unknown to them. In a strange sense, they didn't know what to do with us, except send anything with eye problems over to the clinic. Medical school did little to train MDs on how to handle eye emergencies, so we were the experts. It was a blessing and a curse.

On-call responsibilities started immediately, and in the middle of summer, trauma was present in spades. I learned to hate temperatures above 60 degrees, because it meant people were probably going to be doing stupid things, thereby creating a long night of covering eye emergencies. For the first several weeks, we just shadowed the second year ophthalmology resident when a call came in. That quickly evaporated and the pager was ours. I learned to hate that damn thing. Between the University Hospital trauma service and Kosair Children's Hospital, you averaged about three visits a night to the ER during the summer. Being on call, every third night sapped your strength quickly. You were either on call, pre-call or post-call. The day at work after a night with the pager could be a very long day, because you still had to work your normal clinic day that might last until six or seven PM. If you didn't go to bed the previous night, fatigue wasn't even a fair word to describe your state. You just existed. The days became a blur. Human interaction almost became the enemy. It was the middle of November before I had a night on call where I didn't have to go in to see a patient. Winter and bitter cold temperatures were gifts, because they dramatically dropped the number of trauma victims.

Since we were now the ophthalmology residents, everyone considered us the experts in all things related to eye care. Unfortunately, on day one I knew little more than the ER doctors did. It was an overwhelming feeling to walk into an exam room in the ER and find massive facial trauma with everybody looking at you and asking if the globes were okay. I just wanted to throw my hands up and say, "I don't know!" But I had to figure it out, and if

I couldn't, I had to call the senior resident for help. My seniors hated the first two months of our training, but it was a rite of passage. We had never seen any of these things rolling in the door and questions were everywhere in my mind. Most ophthalmology program directors will tell you it takes at least three weeks for a first year resident to finally be able to generate a good enough view of the back of any eye with our equipment and lenses, before they can fairly decipher what is going on. It takes about three to six months for them to know what that image really means and the management needed to care for the patient. By six months, we had seen most things at least once, and our calls to the backup senior residents became few and far between. The learning curve was massive and unforgiving. You had to figure it out quickly or your nights just became longer. Nobody was going to come in and see your patients for you. Backup was always available, but they were there primarily to handle unusual questions or surgical management of trauma.

Clinical work involved pediatrics, glaucoma, retinal disease, oculoplastics, neuro ophthalmology, cataract evaluations and general care of the eye. The oculoplastic specialists were the experts in caring for trauma around the eye including the bony socket, which holds the eye as well as the eyelids. Our neurophthalmologist helped us with the connection between the brain and eye, which could be damaged due to strokes, trauma along with many other things. For such a tiny organ, volumes of books, magazines and reference sources were published each month to discuss the latest ideas on how to preserve or enhance our vision. The field was incredibly dynamic and filled with some of the brightest minds I had ever met. Innovations were quickly reviewed and adapted if they worked. The public had an insatiable appetite for newer, better, faster, and stronger techniques related to their eyes. I found the contrasting desire to acquire safe eye treatment, with the intense willingness to accept novel ideas like new refractive surgeries, a fascinating study of the human element.

First year residents were expected to ask questions and lean on the attending physician in clinic. They taught us most of the techniques used to examine patients. The second and third year residents, "pushed," the clinic along by seeing the bulk of the patients. Most of our office time was spent caring for the indigent population or veterans. Honestly, they received good care, but at the cost of extended wait times for both appointments and seeing a physician in clinic. There was a huge need in our community. A dose of humility couldn't help but touch your heart, as humanity poured through our doors daily, in an attempt to preserve whatever vision they had left. The pictures in my ophthalmology training books seemed to be sitting in the waiting area every day. I had learned no matter how tired I was, and I was dead most of my first year, you didn't want to miss clinic, or the only example in the city of Louisville of a rare genetic disorder like Choroideremia might just pass through.

Dreaded call and the middle of night calls thankfully slowed during the winter months. We had emergency room consults down to a science to minimize our time in the ER and maximize time in bed. All residents finally get to the point of feeling overworked and under-loved at some point in their training. Patients were keeping us from rest, and you really had to fight the mentality of making them the enemy in the process. Shattered faces and blood became the norm, and by January, you were numbed to some degree. It was mental self-protection, I guess.

The human element came crashing back to me one weekend that winter, however. My annoying pager wailed from the nightstand around 2 am, announcing a consult. University Hospital wanted me to come see a young male who had massive head trauma from a motor vehicle accident (MVA). I was pissed. Fatigue held onto every ounce of my energy I had left, but I got up, put my scrubs on and headed downtown. All I could focus on was how long it would take me to finish the work and get back home before the little black box ruined my night again. The AM station played some bizarre call-in show about aliens and UFOs. I was uninterested, but it was noise and helped keep me awake for the drive. All ophthalmology residents had a bag full of toys, which told the ER world the eye service was here. You just hoped nobody else noticed, so you could escape before someone else wanted a quick consult. I found the ER doctor that called me, and he pointed me to the appropriate bay. I perused the chart quickly and focused on my efficiency. I wanted to sleep. Walking over to the exam bay, I saw it was filled with a young, trauma victim, who was breathing with the help of a ventilation tube, while yards of IV tubes and bags hung above his bed. Certainly, it looked from a distance that he had more to worry about than his eyes right now. The room was also filled with family members. It seemed like dozens of them crowded the tiny space. A tiny curtain provided them little privacy. I tried to walk in and quickly introduce myself as the eye doctor who was there to make sure his eyes were okay. An overwhelmed, teary father approached me with the world on his shoulders. "Is he going to be okay?" he asked. I could only tell him, "The trauma service is managing his care, and he is in good hands. The next 24-48 hours are critical for him. I am the eye doctor and here to look at his eyes." His vision cleared for a moment, and he looked at me and said, "Do you go to St Michael Catholic Church?" I stopped dead in my tracks. I knew this man. Suddenly, the anonymity was gone. The person on the gurney had a name and a family again. I apologized to them for not knowing more, but reassured the family after my exam that his eyes were fine and he was in the best facility for this type of care. I finally left the room, wrote up my findings and disappeared into the pitch-black darkness, ashamed of myself. Months of hard work had hardened my soul. I prayed for forgiveness on the way home and asked for help in rediscovering why I wanted to become a surgeon. My head hit the pillow, but I slept little the rest of the evening. That night affected me for months. I could never again forget that we were caring for someone's loved one. They deserved my best and if I couldn't give it to them, I needed to stop the charade. To this day, every decision I make in the clinic, ER or operating room is made thinking about how I would handle this if it were my own mother or father. It has served me well since and I have finally learned to sleep better.

The rest of the year was filled with lid lacerations, orbital fractures, conjunctivitis and a plethora of other eye ailments.

Fatigue still ruled your world, especially mine, since I was working with about half the amount of hemoglobin everybody else had. My body adapted. By the end of that first year, we were capable residents ready to advance to the next stage of our training. The next set of victims, I mean residents, would be welcomed into the program so they could take our place on call. I had survived probably the worst year of my life, outside of trying to die in 1995 and 1996. I was anxious to find my pillow again.

Chapter 24
A Rough Start

The next set of residents was indoctrinated on July 1st of 2005. I became a second year and more weight fell onto my class' shoulders to do more work in the clinic. A year of training had exposed us to all extremes from tragedy and loss of vision to simple glasses prescriptions. Now, the lingering question was could we learn to fix those problems through medical, laser or surgical management? Thankfully, the burden of call shifted dramatically to the newbies and required my attention only about two or three times a month. To some degree, chronic fatigue eased and I found my family again.

Surgical exposure started in a slow, controlled process to develop skills while minimizing risk to patients. First and second year residents bounced off the walls when a patient showed up with a mature, totally white, cataract and a guarded prognosis. If the patient needed to have the lens removed, it was a match made in heaven for a younger set of hands, with an attending almost remotely piloting the training surgeon. That's when I realized how much this training resembled the flying world.

~

Sheppard AFB, Texas, in 1991 was a buzz of activity. It was a major training base for several enlisted career fields, but what caught your attention was the dozen or more jets in the air over the runway environment at all times of the day. It was the home of the Euro NATO Joint Jet Pilot Training (ENJJPT) program. Its mission was to train fighter pilots for the NATO countries that participated. Everyone there had gone through a rigorous selection process in their own country. Inside the walls of the 80th Flying Training Wing, it was almost like the scattered city of Babel. Every language you could imagine was being spoken in hallways, briefing rooms and offices. Bizarro world meets Texas.

Becky and I arrived, married for only nine months, ready for a busy year. I promised every ounce of energy I had to earn my wings, and she knew how important the coming year was to me. My class was full of Americans, Germans, Italians, Norwegians and a Brit. There was no shortage of egos or personalities. Before we were allowed to start in earnest, though, a full medical exam was required to make sure we would be physically ready for the rigors of flying jets under extreme physical forces. Each body part was examined and possibly reexamined looking for problems. It was nerve wracking. After most of the day had expired, walking from one clinic in the base hospital to the next, we ended up in the flight surgeon's office for the finishing touches. Before leaving and being given the final blessing, a medical technician, dressed in all white scrubs, asked me to take off my shoes and socks. I obliged, but was taken aback by his next step. He pulled out a small poster sized piece of paper with two footprint-sized outlines on it. He retrieved a container of black ink and a small roller. He asked me to sit down and he rolled the black ink on the bottom of my feet as if he was painting a room. I then carefully stood on the paper for a few seconds and sat back down once the prints were captured. Previously, I had fingerprints taken, but this was new. After cleaning my feet, I replaced my socks and shoes before I just had to ask why he wanted footprints. The answer wasn't warm or fuzzy! "Lieutenant, if you pound it in during your training, the small pieces and parts can be hard to identify. Your boots and their contents usually survive reasonably intact. This way we can pull your foot out and make sure it was you," was the tech's response. I sat there dumbfounded for a second and just took in the statement. I walked out and thought, this is serious stuff. From that point forward, most of us never wore our dog tags around our necks on a chain, but instead wove them into the shoelaces of our flight boots, just in case. The footprint lesson would hit way too close to home in the very near future for our entire Wing.

The flight room was active and lively. Initially, we spent several weeks learning aerospace basics like ejections, decompression and parachute landings. While in the altitude chamber, I was the lucky soul taken off oxygen at 32,000 feet. The point was to show us how debilitating and insidious hypoxia was to brain function. Body gases escaped mercifully, as we ascended, until they finally asked me to remove my mask. I was handed a clipboard with simple math problems and tasks on it. I quickly worked through a page of problems before slipping away about a minute later. The clipboard fell into my lap, and I stared blankly off in the distance. Numerous attempts by the staff to bring me back to reality were useless. Finally, somebody put my mask back on, which resulted in an immediate physiologic deep breath. I resumed work on the clipboard without missing a beat. I was amnesic to what had just happened. My classmates responded with a thunderous laugh as I recovered. My blue lips and fingernails rapidly returned to their normal pink color. That exhibition left no doubt in any of our minds that hypoxia was dangerous or even lethal.

We finally arrived on the flight line and replaced the class six months ahead of us in school. They were headed to supersonic T-38 training the next day. Envy was probably present to some degree, but we were within days of starting our own jet training in the more forgiving T-37. We worked to learn our new routines of getting to the flight line on early days around 4:30 or 5 am and how to handle the dreaded morning briefings. Emergency procedures were reviewed before starting every single flying period, and if you were deemed deficient, you didn't fly. The stress in the morning's flight room was palpable, because one of us would be called to stand up and handle a given emergency. Other victims were likely to follow. Reputations were made or broken during these sessions.

The day after hitting the flight line, I arrived ready to take on the world. A giant cloud of black smoke rose from the runway area next to some large fuel tanks. I wondered what was going on, but I was too busy to rubberneck. As I entered the Flying Wing, the doors were suddenly locked behind me, and I was told to stay away from the phones. "What's going on?" I asked. The person said, "A T-38 just went down next to the runway and all external communications are shut down until further notice." Common cell phone technology hadn't arrived in the world yet. I walked to the flight room, wondering if Becky had any idea what had happened on base. I certainly didn't want her worrying about my safety. When I finally found my classmates, they looked shell-shocked. One of the American students in the class we just met and replaced yesterday had died just minutes ago on his dollar ride, or first ride in a T-38, with an Italian instructor in the backseat. I knew what I wanted to do was risky, but this brought the intensity of my new world very close to an unexpected crescendo. It also reemphasized the point that I had to be as prepared as possible to minimize my chances of dying from pilot error. Unconsciously, I looked down to make sure my boots were on tight, and the dog tags still present. Remnants of the leftover ink had finally worn away from the tiny cracks in the soles of my feet, but not the memory of why it was there.

Several days later, the young man was laid to rest, and a formation of T-38s flew overhead of the assembled Wing on the vast concrete tarmac. Our jets rested quietly except the group in poignant missing man formation. I hardly knew the guy, but I softly cried with the rest of the most testosterone-driven group of people I had ever known. This really was dangerous.

~

Certain surgical skills were only acquired through practice and I was determined to perfect mine. I probably underestimated the effort required to learn many of them. I wasn't about to be lazy in my approach, though. Every two or three weeks, I visited the local pig slaughterhouse to pick up a bag of pig eyes for training. After making a call early in the morning, I arrived at their front gate around lunch to meet one of the employees looking for a quick break. They walked across the parking lot in a bloodstained, white apron carrying a clear plastic bag full of dozens of eyes. We would exchange pleasantries and then I climbed back in my car with my goodies. It felt almost illegal. For the next week or so, I remained after work to practice suturing, wound creation, injections or anything else I could dream up which might mimic our work in the operating room. After ten days or so, the bag had to be removed from the lab refrigerator and disposed of due to its smell. It was a sordid routine.

Meredith and Colin were always curious about what I was doing all day. I invited them to join me in the lab occasionally in the evenings. They entertained me with their fascinating dissections, but they were most thrilled by their new school-like activity, which didn't require a write-up or lesson plan. It was pure unadulterated fun for them. I found more time to develop those desperately needed skills while getting a rare opportunity to see my kid's smiles. They were now becoming young people with maturing desires and personalities. I treasured those moments.

While manning one of our eye clinics, I was finally given a cataract case of my own. Inside, I was thrilled with the opportunity, but still scared to death. Had all that practice prepared me enough to handle the case? Extra pig eyes had to be ordered to make sure. When my surgical day arrived, I reviewed the plan with my attending. The patient had extensive damage to their eyes from poorly controlled diabetes, and they now had an advanced cataract. I had seen every step of this surgery dozens of times, but this was one of the first times I had the lead role. Prepping and draping the patient was a simple, yet routine process, but now it became arduous, as I struggled through the details. Eyelids were opened with a lid speculum, and the microscope moved into position with its sun-like intensity illuminating the field. Basic entrance wounds were made and injections followed to maintain the shape of the eye throughout the procedure. So far so good. As I made the initial stab into the cataract to open the front capsule, it split in half almost like a piece of popcorn opening. I had never seen that before and neither had my boss. The almost mature cataract was swollen and when I gave it the opening, it had no interest in going quietly. The next two and a half hours were a wrestling match. When it was finished, an artificial lens was in place as planned, but the surgical eye would need significant time to recover. It really wasn't my fault, but I left the OR that day exhausted and mentally beaten up. Fortunately, time was a wonderful healer to my patient's eye and me. He went on to develop good vision again, and I slowly gained confidence through more cases. My mind and hands were finding their way after a rough beginning, but I thought I could see the light at the end of the tunnel.

Our second year of residency ended after we had performed dozens of laser procedures, seen countless patients and performed maybe a dozen eye surgeries. The last year sat ready for us to arrive and promised the bulk of our surgical training. Attendings now looked to Jon Sohn, Shunai Jiang and myself to carry the torch into our third year. We were now the senior residents and expected to handle cases, while educating our junior doctors.

Finally, I could taste the end. Could God's strength push me across the finish line?

~

Brutal early mornings brought more emergency scenarios and a strict flight routine. Preflight required a thorough review of the mission you were about to fly. We had memorized pages of numbers, bold face lists of emergency responses and other checklists to run through from the initial aircraft checkout to post flight recovery. Making every possible step as habitual as possible minimized mistakes. We couldn't tolerate forgetting steps since it might result in loss of aircraft or even life. After meeting with our instructor pilot for the morning ride, we progressed to the life support room to collect our helmets, gloves, parachutes and flight bags. A quick check of our oxygen masks on our way out the door ensured one of our most crucial pieces of equipment was in working order. Blue Air Force crew vans constantly circled between the immense, concrete space with white jets arrayed in an orderly fashion on the tarmac and the operations building. You took your seat quickly inside the vehicle. Instructors bantered back and forth, due to their boredom from the routine, while most students had mission plans streaming through their head. Before flights, my brain almost felt like a NASCAR race from the breakneck thoughts crashing into each other. In the beginning, an instructor told me that God gave your brain a dollar to fly with. You start using 99 cents of that dollar to just move the stick back and forth and only 1 cent to think about what the hell you are supposed to be doing. As you matured, eventually 99 cents was used to look outside, mission plan and be situationally aware, while only 1 cent was needed to think about the physical act of moving the airplane around. He couldn't have been more right.

Leaving the van, your job shifted to making sure your airplane was ready to fly. Inside and outside, checks were made in the same order every time with a crew chief outside ensuring everything was ready. Radio calls for taxi permission finally got the show and you moving to the end of the runway. Once clearance was given, a series of verbal checks were made, followed by pushing the throttles to their maximum setting. Your heart raced as the increasing airflow started to tug the little jet off the ground. More checks, radio calls, departures patterns, gear and flap retraction before you were headed into the heavens for the meat of the work. The next fifty or so minutes were spent completing the required syllabus of training. You were graded on every step you made. A reversal of all those steps brought you back home and into the flight room for a critique of your skills. Bubble critic sheets were filled out and either preparation for another flight, class work or the next day's training began immediately. The Air Force expected a total commitment of your time during this year. Either they got it or you went home.

In the first week, I was so intimidated by the flying and the possibility of passing out, G-locking, from lack of blood flow to the brain during high force maneuvers, that I constantly squeezed my abdomen and legs as I was instructed in the aerospace course. The problem was that I was barely undergoing any force at all most of the time and was wearing myself out. An instructor from the Netherlands was so fed up with me that he unhooked his harness in the middle of a flight and almost climbed into my seat to scream in my face. "Stop squeezing," he yelled. Frustrated, he returned to his ejection seat, strapped back in and started teaching again. Message heard loud and clear. I finally started to relax, and the queasiness I felt from being tossed around like a ragdoll during maneuvers disappeared into the hot Texas sky as well.

Check rides were the culmination of a section of training, where an evaluator would take you from beginning to end on a predetermined mission. A grade was given and if satisfactory, you moved on to the next set of exercises. So far, I had progressed very well and had developed a reputation of knowing my stuff and having solid hands. I was nervous about my first check ride and I became increasingly anxious based on the current weather. We became amateur meteorologists because our daily routine revolved around whether we could fly or not. My day to check called for scattered thunderstorms and heavy cloud cover all day. It looked almost certain to wash us out. I was praying for another prettier day until word finally came across that a few of us were going to fly. A quick look outside caused my mind to panic, because I had yet to fly in weather this bad. My flight had to involve spins and high G maneuvers in order to complete the check ride. It would be a chore to find enough space between clouds for all the things planned. There would also likely be no ground or sky references to orient yourself.

I met with my evaluator and we proceeded through our normal routine. His critical eyes watched for my mistakes as we taxied to the runway for takeoff. A dash down the long strip led us into a grey, ugly day. Initially, I flew to an auxiliary field for touch and goes before finally beginning the climb into the mess above. So far, so good, but now was when the flying was about to become exponentially more difficult. He understood this was a challenging environment and tried to help me find places between clouds so I could finish the flight. After another 30 minutes, we had gratefully completed the curriculum. I turned for home. Horrible luck stumbled into the cockpit when I looked at the attitude indicator. It told us which way was up or down, and at that moment it was tumbling. My inexperience felt it needed to be reset. It was a common reaction to fix everything before taking the next step. The rub was that would take about a minute to complete, and I didn't have the space or more importantly the gas to turn away from home. My initial attempt to turn away was met with a stern order to point the nose at Sheppard AFB. We could see the ground and I was at Bingo fuel. That is the amount of gas required to land before going dry. I sensed the major mistake and the cockpit became my personal sauna.

Back in the evaluator's office, I was quizzed for another half an hour on various topics before my personal instructor was retrieved from our flight room. As he entered our area, my heart sank. I had hooked (failed) the ride. So much for the illustrious beginning. Both of them actually spent time complimenting me on my skills, but he couldn't pass me due to my lack of airmanship, and that could have caused us not to make it home. I was crushed.

The next six months, I picked up steam, and I never failed another ride in the program. I even became an excellent instrument pilot due to my attention to detail. I wonder if God was making sure, He taught me a simple, but hard lesson that day so I couldn't forget the basics. The last seven months of flight training would be in the supersonic T-38 Talon, and all of us were chomping at the bit to ride this high performance trainer. It would prepare us for the fighter world. Mentally I had a hard time letting go of that early error though. My obsessive-compulsive personality was running full speed.

Chapter 25

Skills, Fear and Anger

The annual rite of passage occurred as scheduled on July 1st of 2006, when the next group of victims entered their residency training and everybody else moved up or graduated to the real world. That meant the heat of the summer and trauma was in full bloom. The first several weeks of my last year of training were painful again due to a bounty of calls from the learning doctors. I was okay with it, because I distinctly remembered how intimidating the first couple of months were when everything under the sun was being thrown at you as the "eye expert." I also had the great blessing of Dr. Todd Purkiss being my second year resident in the clinic. He was bright, motivated and worked extremely hard to take great care of patients. Between the two of us, we could manage our assigned clinical load, and he also helped instruct the new guys.

Lid lacerations, ruptured globes and orbital fractures were earned over the weekends like presents at a birthday party. The oculoplastic service was always scrambling to meet the need. It meant more training and cases for third year residents, and it was why we suffered through the challenging first two years of our ophthalmology residency.

As the number of cases under your belt grew, so did your skills and confidence. Within two months, I had a reasonable handle on removing routine cataracts. Most of the time, what you see in a training program is anything but routine, though.

Pathology walked into our clinics daily, which I had never seen since and may never see again. Our patient population just didn't come for an exam unless they couldn't function. Maybe that is an exaggeration, but not by much. Preventive care was a foreign concept, due to either financial constraints or lack of exposure to the benefits of routine medical visits.

I had always dreamed that my most memorable case would involve taking a hopeless eye and making it 20/20. I was wrong. About four months into my last year, my attending, Dr. Judith Mohay, told me we were going to tackle a longtime patient's cataract nobody wanted to do. There was good reason. The patient had sarcoidosis, an autoimmune disease, and it had affected multiple organ systems in her body and it had especially wrecked her eyes. Eventually, she developed such bad cataracts from the intraocular inflammation that we couldn't see the back of her eyes anymore. She was cane tapping blind. Dr. Mohay was our angel and so committed to caring for every patient as if they were her children. We loved her, and she loved us back. When she said I needed to do the case, I didn't bat an eye until I took a further look and wondered if I was about to step into a disaster again. We took the patient to the operating room and performed all the routine prep work to get the eye ready. On entering the eye, all was quiet on the Western Front until I tried to get to the lens. A dense membrane had formed over the pupil and my sharp instrument couldn't even poke a hole in it. Improvising, we found a pair of long nosed scissors to cut away the scar tissue. It was tedious work, but now we had access to the lens. The mature white lens reminded me of the nightmare case I tackled just one year ago. I wondered if abandoning our pursuit was the better part of valor, but we were now committed. Careful removal and decompression of the swollen mature lens allowed us to use modern techniques and phacoemulsification, an instrument that breaks up lenses using a tiny high frequency jackhammer. Slow and steady wins the race in this case and after 45 minutes, a beautiful new lens was in place, and the eye wound was closed. We really had no idea what to expect 24 hours later when she would come for her first post-operative visit.

The next day, a steady flow of work kept us busy all morning until lunchtime. Once the last patient was seen, we headed down the hall to leave the building for lunch. That's when I noticed my surgery patient waiting in the front lobby. She was over an hour early. You could always spot her before, due to her white cane that guided her around town. I approached her and verbally introduced myself, but she quickly stopped me and said, "I can see, I can see!" Tears rolled down her face. She was so excited that she came extra early to take in the world. I couldn't let her sit there for an hour while I ate, so I offered my arm to escort her back for the quick first day post-op exam. She smacked it away and repeated, "I can see." We slowly walked down the long hall together as she gathered in sights that were hidden from her for years. Her voice trembled as we talked.

In the exam lane, I anxiously settled her into the chair and brought up the eye chart. I advanced the letters to fairly small lines with great expectations. She couldn't read them. Finally, I backed off and placed successively larger lines before her until she could read the big E. She was 20/400. My shoulders slumped. I was so disappointed, but I looked over at her in the dimly lit exam lane, and I could still make out the tears continuing to spill onto her cheeks. Her life had been transformed yesterday, and I had failed to understand how important a gift we were able to give her. She could now clean her house, fix her own food and walk down the street to the local store, all without assistance. In other words, she could function at a whole new level, much like she did five or ten years ago. The retina in the back of her eyes was a mess. She would probably never see better than this, but for now, I took in the special moment. My attendings had helped me develop skills to preserve the most precious human sense; sight.

From that day forward, I looked at the day after surgery as Christmas Day. It was an instance to witness what God had kept me around for all these years. Every experience and every patient is different, but I still feel like a little kid when I enter the exam lane to unwrap the present. Only they are not your presents, they are your gifts to others. I always take pause and thank God. Now before doing any cases, I stop briefly, usually outside the operating room before each case, and quietly pray that my knowledge and hands will allow me to restore their vision. I ask that He allow me to become a magnifier of his Grace!

~

Winters in Texas were typically pretty mild, but they brought with them an awesome aid to the fliers on base, cold dense air! Aircraft jet engine and aerodynamic performance was significantly enhanced when operated in colder weather. Our class had just finished the first half of our training and was headed across the hall to a new flight room and instructors. Watching the high performance T-38s streaking across the sky for six months had us aching for the chance to strap on this jet. In the back of my mind, I couldn't help but think of the fatal accident just six months ago.

Most of our instructors were veterans of the Persian Gulf War and stories flowed freely, especially on Friday nights at the Officers Club after a couple of beers. We soaked it all in. By comparison, modern fighter jets are far faster and more powerful, but this was a major upgrade from the thick winged T-37, and its pedestrian speeds. Routines really didn't change much. The major adjustment was going to be adapting to higher G forces along with landing speeds that exceeded 160 knots. The T-37 could be landed below 70 knots, if it was light on gas.

Our flight room continued to amuse and entertain due to the diversity of personalities overfilling the space. I learned to curse in multiple languages. I was convinced the Italians hated each other every morning due to their lively arm waving and loud discussions. Their culture caused me to chuckle several times a day.

Training involved aerobatics, instruments, low level and formation flying. Each skill was unique and required intense focus to do things correctly. Our airplanes were built around 1960 and the avionics were designed with old, but proven, technology. We didn't have GPS receivers or CRT displays to guide us. Old-fashioned techniques to navigate had to be mastered in case all that fancy technology failed you flying an F-16 in enemy territory.

Mental processing had to pick up dramatically in this phase or the pace of the airplane would leave you behind. This segment of training is where you saw young pilots sink or swim.

Just two or three months into T-38s, I became deathly sick. A wicked sore throat, fever, chills and swollen glands shut me down. I spent days on the couch. Multiple visits to the ER and the flight surgeon couldn't generate a diagnosis. The medical staff was baffled and loaded me up on antibiotics, but my symptoms only continued to worsen. Finally, the third mono test came back positive, and I was told to go home and wait it out. At that point, it looked inevitable I would wash back into the class behind me. I was frustrated, but felt so bad that I just wanted to go back to my couch and sleep. After about ten days, my throat improved dramatically, and I was able to increase my fluid and solid intake to fairly normal levels. I approached the flight surgeon about going back to the flight line. He sent me back to work, and I walked into the flight room with a silly grin, asking to be put on the schedule. Staying in my class meant a daunting schedule to bring me back up to speed with the rest of my buddies. In fact, it meant I would probably have to "double bang," fly twice a day, for weeks. That could be the kiss of death or a true gift to my flying career. If I struggled to deal with the explosive, increased pace, I might become overwhelmed and wash out of the program. However, if I could handle it, getting to fly twice a day was the greatest way to build skills quickly. I wanted to press forward.

That night, my flight was scheduled to do one of our rare night flights, and this one was also in a formation with another jet. I was jumping directly into the fire on the first ride. I hadn't flown in over two weeks and now was trying to remind myself how to run through the checklists. Flying at night would become commonplace in the real world, but for students, it added an additional level of difficulty. Instruments were harder to read, ground landmarks were difficult to discern and your wingman's position was challenging to judge due to the decreased amount of visual cues present.

I was one of the last groups to takeoff and I led the two ship, two airplanes in formation, into the air and on our way south of Wichita Falls, Texas. We were fortunate to be allowed by Fort Worth Center controllers to do the "Dallas Tour," due to the late hour. That meant we were allowed to fly directly over downtown Dallas at a designated altitude in formation until we requested the return to Sheppard. I was thirty minutes into my first flight in weeks and stress mixed with exhilaration for our multiple passes over the skyscrapers. I eventually passed the lead to my wingman, and we took in the sights for a few more minutes before flying back home. Flying three feet from another jet at night is intense, especially when you haven't flown for a while. My skills were rusty, but I survived and landed back home without scaring the instructor in the backseat. I was back, and hoping the coming weeks would re-sharpen my talent.

Reality and rumors were also mixing together in an ugly political mixture over our future assignments. President Bill Clinton was taking significant swipes at military funding, and all the services were bracing for painful changes. In the flying world, squadrons were being retired along with many airframes. The bottom line was flying jobs were being lost at a rapid rate and experienced fighters were being shoved out of their service with little fanfare. It meant ENJJPT may not be able to even give us flying jobs, much less fighter slots at the end of our training, after spending a million dollars to put wings on our chest. We just figured the worst would pass before our assignment night came. Our timing couldn't have turned out any worse.

~

For the rest of my last year of residency training, I focused on becoming the best surgeon I could be and completed numerous glaucoma, oculoplastic and retina surgeries. Each work was meticulous in its own way. Details were paramount to maximize outcomes for your patients. It was stressful, but exhilarating. Our attendings went to great lengths to make sure we were not only technically competent, but also excellent doctors with our patients' best interest as our first priority. My personal experiences dealing with multiple life threatening illnesses appreciated their effort and guidance.

As always, my health was a glory hog and couldn't stand to be out of the limelight. In early 2007, I developed tea colored urine, and it was worrisome for blood. Immediately, I went to see a local urologist for an exam. There was serious concern that the mass had finally invaded my urinary collecting system, or even the kidney. Urine tests and bladder scopes gave no real answers, except to announce a lot of inflammatory cells were present in my urine. I was referred down to Anderson for their urology oncologist to evaluate and scope me up to the kidney. My mind once again could only entertain devastating news. Could this bring the whole show down, just months short of the finish line? Anxiety just retook its stately position among our ranks.

My dad and I jumped on an airplane for the procedure. He was always so positive, but sometimes a bit naïve. We enjoyed meals and some movies together before seeing the doctor and having the scope. The procedure didn't last long and he came out to tell my father that there was no evidence of malignancy, but inflammation was likely present from the pressure exerted by the beast next door to the kidney. Few things seemed to be described in absolutes with regard to my health. I lived in a gray world. Dad exhaled and waited for me to go to recovery. His phone was overheating from the rapid-fire calls he was making to tell the world. When my head cleared from the anesthesia, he hugged me in bed and said it was going to be okay. I looked up and smiled, until I realized I needed to go to the bathroom. That meant using the same pathway a whole bunch of ugly instruments had just retreated from. I cringed, but reached for the urinal. My dad pulled the curtain, but he should have shoved a towel into my mouth. I struggled to contain the screaming that obviously wanted to be released, as a few drops found their way out. It hurt like hell, and for the next 24 hours, I dreaded trips to the bathroom. Of course, the advice from the nursing staff was drink lots of fluid. I looked at them as if they were smoking dope. I wasn't sure I could accept their instruction.

We returned, knowing that inflammation was the only cause of my hematuria. I tried to limit sodas or anything else that might inflame the urinary system. Over the coming weeks, all systems returned to their standard abnormal state. Another bullet dodged, but I was starting to feel like the lady on the spinning wheel at a carnival with a guy throwing knives at me. How long before he didn't miss?

It was now time to start looking for a job as a general ophthalmologist. I collected leads from various people around town and sent out letters asking to see if anybody was interested. Several practices responded. One was a very short drive out of town and seemed very promising. Becky and I investigated the area for houses, schools and took a serious look at the practice to include finances. A contractual offer was made and my brother approved of the terms. I was ready to jump in with both feet until a bomb went off in the room. A memorandum of agreement was sent to me, laying out the terms under which I could buy into the practice. It was short and sweet, except for the rancid pill sitting in the last sentence. It stated that if I left the practice, became sick or died, the other owner could buy my share for $1. I dropped the paper to the ground. I picked it up again and reread it. Yep, that is what it said. I had never hidden my health issues from anybody over the previous 14 years, and for that statement to be present, it was a clear deal breaker. I walked away in shock.

Other options were available in the local area and I finally started talking seriously with a single practicing ophthalmologist. He was very interested in growing and he had received solid recommendations about me from one of my attendings. After several visits, a contract was worked out that set up a long-term relationship. I was thrilled. I was also ignoring one of the warning signs given out frequently to new doctors looking for work. There usually is a reason why a doctor has been by themselves in practice for over a decade and control is the likely culprit. I didn't care. I buried my head and signed away.

~

It is hard to describe the thrill of putting a fast-moving jet through its paces. Near the end of our training, we were doing two ship low-level formations. It required detailed plans, maps and weather briefs to get it right. If you and your wingman were on the same page, it was ecstasy. Multiple low levels routes were available around Sheppard and on one particular day, I remember we had a southerly route that would take us just north of the Dallas-Ft Worth area. Maps were drawn up by hand, with turn points picked out due to our ability to find them and stay inside the designated military flight route. In the morning, winds were applied, just before stepping to the jet, to correct the headings needed for the course planned. There was no such thing as GPS or inertial guidance to shepherd our progression. This was the old-fashioned way of doing things. Map, clock, ground. The stopwatch on your wrist was your best or worst friend. You had better not screw up your timing device, or Lord help you. We took off as a formation, but spread as far apart on the runway as possible for safety reasons. Quickly, we joined up to three feet fingertip formation and headed to our area. As my flight approached the course, we descended to 500 feet where buildings, towers, creeks and roads were visible from your position for several seconds. If you were a mile left or right of where you planned, you likely would never find that turn point. It was intense. My eyeballs hurt from the constant staring and scanning. Map, clock, ground. Getting lost on the ride resulted in a pissed off instructor yelling from the backseat. I felt like my hair was on fire most of the time, as I struggled to keep from becoming task saturated. Everything was crosschecked rapidly, as the world whizzed by just under your boots. The final run was even more fun, because your wingman would tuck in behind you from his lateral, one mile away, tactical position, and the throttles were pushed up until you hit 400 knots. For the next 45 seconds, nothing in the world touched a neuronal connection in your brain. All circuits were focused on what was happening right in front of you, and the jet in your hands. Crossing the final target, you pulled up out of the weeds and breathed again. For a student pilot, this was about as good as it gets.

The trip home had one more thrill in store before putting the plane back in the chocks for another lucky person to take it out for a spin. Overhead patterns were among my favorite things to do in T-38 training. It was a 3-D puzzle of airplanes, all obeying a very strict set of rules, but vying for airspace and runway time to do landings. We meshed together like a beehive in what seemed chaotic to everybody except us. As I came up initial, flying straight down the runway from 1500 feet altitude, with my wingman just a couple of feet away in fingertip formation, I yanked the jet into a steep level turn shortly after crossing the runway threshold. My partner counted to three and did the same. From that point forward, each plane was on its own. The supersonic trainer's wings talked to you like an old man. Under high G's and near stall speeds, they creaked and groaned, making it feel as if somebody was outside jumping on the wings. Disconcerting the first time you experienced it, but once you understood how hard the vibrations were, you knew how much room you had before bad things would happen. Rolling out of the turn and parallel to the runway, but now going the opposite direction, the gear and flaps had to be put down. Spatial awareness was a must to maintain proper distance from other airplanes and ensure you didn't overshoot the runway due to winds. It was the coolest game. When you reached the perch, a point where you would start a descending turn for a final approach and landing, proper planning set you up to hopefully roll out on the runway at a safe height. Landing around 165 knots always had your attention. Driving the plane down, until you couldn't stand it anymore, and flaring gave you the satisfaction of putting the jet through its paces. If you had more gas, more touch and goes were a must. The instructor in the back seat always appreciated a chance to put his hands on the stick and show his prowess as well. If it didn't feel like elephants were about to dance on the wings during each pattern, your buddies on the ground or the instructor in the back were likely to verbally blast your efforts. This world was all about bravado. Man, was it thrilling!

Over a year's worth of intense training was finishing and the American students' expectations for assignments was hitting an all-time low at Sheppard in June of 1992. The fighter era was put on hold as our Assignment Night hit. Many of our instructors with actual mission experience during the Persian Gulf War were being forced out of the service or they were told to go to a bad assignment without their family. Twenty-four hours before we were allowed to pick our next training, the list of jets and our class ranking was released. On that list, I was fortunate enough to have the top pick in the class. Our assignments did not have a single fighter assignment. ENJJPT typically gave fighter jobs to all of its graduates with few exceptions, but our class was offered one instructor pilot job, a bunch of big airplanes and the remaining one third of the class was sent to a desk job for the next four years. We were told it was coming, but we were stunned when it hit us in the face like a truck. As a captain, my career couldn't wait around four years in a non-flying job. I had already done that in the space community. Becoming an instructor pilot at a pilot training base would not set the table to become promotable at this point in my life. I had no choice but accept an assignment flying big airplanes. To say I was bitter was an understatement. I tried to keep my head up, but I couldn't believe how screwed up things had become. That night, we still celebrated wildly as a group, but I couldn't help but wonder, "What if?" The best pilot in our class, Lieutenant David Lynch, wanted a fighter jet so badly that he made the risky move of choosing a banked fighter slot, meaning a desk job for four years with the hopes the Air Force would keep a promise and deliver his dream assignment down the road. The move was a dicey one to make, but after a long wait, it was finally rewarded with an F-15.

Despite the disappointment with our assignments, graduation from Air Force Pilot Training was a treasured moment, when you enter a rare fraternity of dedicated fliers. Becky was seven months pregnant with Meredith when it came time to pin on my wings. I shared with her the story of the Broken Wing Ceremony. It became a symbol of good luck for Army Air Corps pilots during World War II to break their first set of wings. The pilot would keep one half and the other was given to someone dear in their lives. That set of wings was never to be rejoined as long as that pilot was alive. In an otherwise joyous moment, we hugged, kissed and cried, hoping never to have to worry about completing the cycle anytime soon. We were ready to become parents and grab life by the horns.

As it turned out, I was diagnosed with cancer just two and a half years later. I saw the world in that time and truly enjoyed the dedicated people and missions we flew in the heavy airlift world. God knew something was coming and helped maximize my flying before the bottom fell out.

Before that could happen, my father was a proud as a peacock of his two sons who were working hard to climb the ladder of success. He was running the general store and baking pizzas in a rural area just outside of Elizabethtown, Kentucky. I decided to give him a framed picture of the two trainers I flew at ENJJPT along with a set of wings in the middle recessed into the mat. It was sharp and he smartly took it back to his upstairs bedroom in the store to enjoy. That is, of course, after doing some bragging about where they came from. Just months later, he would wake in the middle of the night with the smoke detector blaring a God awful noise and noticed his room was filled with smoke. He attempted to run down the stairs, but found a wall of flames licking its way up the stairwell. There was no way out, except through a second floor window. Little time remained as the 150-year-old dry, tinder box was primed for the moment to become a distant memory for everybody who knew the building. My dad opened the window and just prior to jumping, saw the picture frame with a set of my wings in it and threw it out in front of him. I'm not sure who took the worst of it, but he survived the fall with some leg injuries as he gathered the broken frame and stepped away from his labor in love. By now, a burning inferno was filling the dark sky with intense radiant heat and flames reaching for the heavens. When assistance arrived, there was nothing to save. The old farmhouse was gone in the blink of an eye and a hardworking man had lost a dear friend. Insurance paid little on the loss and he moved back to Louisville to restart life again in Jeffersontown. We would joke later that he was hoping for a miracle ride on a magic carpet or a set of wings that might suddenly take flight and save him from the jump. Neither happened that night, but we are thrilled to have him still with us. The wings were reframed and still sit proudly displayed in his home. Everything else was bulldozed over into the blackened carbon pit and an era in his life simply disappeared.

~

After eleven years of training to become a doctor, graduation day gracefully arrived for my ophthalmology residency class and me. Each of us had stories of past hardships to share and many tears were shed. It seemed impossible that so much time had passed and finally we were fully trained to care for patients as attending physicians. I approached the podium that night to receive my training diploma with a box of tissue. I knew this was going to be emotional. Once again, I had a hard time keeping my thoughts and emotions together as I went around the room sharing stories of what so many of those present had done for me. Becky, Meredith, Colin and my parents were also there. I cried and blew my nose unabashedly for twenty minutes. By the end, they knew how I felt about the opportunity given to me. Dr. Kaplan and Dr. Joern Soltau had offered a desperate man with multiple medical problems and the internal drive to do something special with his life a chance to train in their department. I was grateful. However, the final glance at my family was what brought me to my knees, as I recalled the death sentences given, but not actually delivered, due to their love and support. God had to be smiling. Eventually, I finally shut up, hugged my family and handed out dozens of bottles of wine to celebrate. Only then, did a smile hit my face. The craziest, stupidest thing I had ever set forth to do was finally accomplished. We had made it!

Chapter 26

The Real World

Private practice was a completely different world from everything I had seen in all my years of medical training. Staff stepped forward to help move things along and did the little steps, so all I had to do was introduce myself, complete the exam and decide on a plan of attack. At first, it rather made me feel uncomfortable, because I was used to doing everything for myself. As time moved on, though, I learned to accept all the assistance, but I never forgot to say thank you. It was part of my culture.

Initially, going to work for another ophthalmologist in town seemed like it was going to work out exceedingly well. We shared call, went to different offices, and I could call if I had questions. The staff was professional and gifted at what they did. I really enjoyed the people I had around me. My schedule was growing steadily, and I spent a half a day a week visiting various primary care physicians trying to build referral patterns. I became the king of mugs, pens and business cards. My trunk was full of them for office visits. By the end of the first year, I had met volumes of doctors that might refer to the office. We even decided to open an office in an adjacent more rural county, because no other ophthalmology practice in Louisville served their needs. For six months, I beat the bushes, developing that side of the business and operating at their local hospital. It was turning into a real opportunity for success. Ophthalmology happens to be one of the most competitive medical fields in Louisville and advertising can be a huge part of the budget for larger groups. With little competition in that county, new patients were coming out of the woodwork.

Problems started to creep into our business relationship during the last year of our agreement though. As we moved closer to becoming partners as stated in my contract, he repeatedly tried to convince me that I wasn't ready for partnership. He was also convinced I wasn't spending enough time out trying to build business relationships. I knew we were headed for a rocky landing when his office manager told me on several occasions that she didn't think he was ready for a partner. She shared her feelings with him as well. He wouldn't hear of it, and when decisions had to be made, it was his kingdom. One morning, he rushed into the office to confront me, because I had scheduled a vacation day for the following week to take my daughter on a college visit. I knew then, becoming partners with him was probably not a healthy endeavor. He complained bitterly that I was unprofessional for giving so little notice. Despite all my medical issues, periodic GI bleeds and the need to visit Anderson for annual checkups, I had never taken a single sick day in two years. His control issues were pouring out everywhere now. In spite of multiple meetings to work out some type of working relationship, he wouldn't contractually agree to any of the verbal promises he was making. We went our separate ways ten days later when my contract expired.

This development shouldn't have come as a surprise, considering how the last six months had gone, but it did. I now had some critical decisions to make about practicing medicine. I could go out, borrow a bunch of money and start my own practice, or try to find a different group to work with. For about ten days, there were a frenzied number of phone calls made, people to meet, bank forms to fill out and corporation licensing documents to file, if I ultimately decided to start fresh on my own. The major hang-up to everything was cash flow. Insurance companies require specific numbers for every physician in their plans, and paperwork could take months. That reality meant living off savings and paying staff from loans, until things caught up. I fiercely debated my options, but after talking at length with my friend, Mike Dahlem, we decided my health made taking out significant loans an unattractive or maybe even dangerous decision for my family.

My focus took a major shift and I re-contacted practices around the city. One doctor, Brennan Greene, had staffed me doing surgeries during my residency. I loved his demeanor and reputation. Off the cuff, I called him and asked if his practice had any interest in bringing on another surgeon. He told me he would look into it and within 30 minutes, his business manager, Mark Prussian, called me. We talked for a while and eventually set up a meeting. I met the other two partners, Dr. Sean Murphy and Dr. John Meyer as well as Dr. Brennan Greene, and I could tell the room was filled with a genuine desire to see if we could make it work. They promised to help me with obtaining insurance numbers, even if I decided not to join their practice.

For the next several days, I felt like an undercover investigator, asking everybody I could think of about the Eye Care Institute and their doctors. I certainly didn't want to make the same ugly mistake twice. Surgical technicians, nurses, primary care doctors and other ophthalmologists all told me the same thing; these were great doctors, who took wonderful care of their patients. I was sold, if we could make the contract work. I made sure they were aware of my health issues, and three days later, I joined the Eye Care Institute. Now, as I look back, I can clearly see a group of people working side-by-side with me, who carry my same value system for patient care. Restoring or maintaining vision is the priority from the front desk to the physicians. My opinion is valued in our meetings and they have never wavered in their support for my health needs, despite some significant new issues. I was meant to be there. It was a puzzling and circuitous route, but my professional life had finally found a home. I was truly grateful.

Over the next several years, my health took several major hits, as I developed liver metastasis and suffered more GI bleeds. MD Anderson, who had been caring for me for over 15 years, finally threw their hands in the air and said they didn't know what to do with me. Becky and I cried ourselves to sleep that night in Houston after my sarcoma specialist decided he had no other options. We were dead in the water.

When we returned to Louisville, I had already been in contact with an interventional radiologist, Dr. Doug Coldwell, who had arrived recently to take over the program at the University of Louisville. He wanted to look at my scans. With little expectation, I was willing to see what he thought. Two different interventional doctors had already tried to map the vascular supply during my odyssey and called it an impossible job. Dr. Coldwell called me a day later and said, "I think I can help you." I eventually picked myself up off the floor and tried to give into the possibility, there was still a chance to deal with the seemingly impossible problems.

Dr. Coldwell had an engineering degree and trained at MD Anderson during the eighties. How did he end up in my corner of the world? Our personalities and thought processes matched up perfectly. We discussed technical issues and ideas like two mechanics trying to figure out how to get an old car running again. I didn't know his vascular world, but he helped me understand his logic. My mind was driven by the stuff. His painstaking planning prepared the way for a possible treatment. A thorough angiogram was done, followed by nuclear studies to make sure nothing he did would cause catastrophic damage to other organs. Everything was coming together and he finally told me on the table, "I've found my way in!" Another impossible task solved by a beautiful angel. My abdominal vascular supply was like a bowl of spaghetti, and he had mapped his way around like a detective. I wanted to kiss him.

A week later, he started the long process of multiple embolization treatments. All were incredibly successful. Scan after scan proved his ability to kill tumor tissue, but more spots came. It was like being in a batting cage with endless balls being fired. Dr. Coldwell never tired and kept me in the game. To this day, Anderson still has no better answers, and my health sits atop a rickety old fence waiting for a collapse that so far hasn't come. All I can imagine is God still has plans for me to do something special. The VA staff in Louisville was very good in supporting my medication needs as well as scans, as the problems became more complicated.

Despite the uncertainty, our family surges forward in life. Meredith has gone on to my beloved alma mater at Purdue University to study nursing on a Navy ROTC scholarship and is thriving. I even had the great privilege of awarding her that scholarship at her high school award ceremony just prior to her graduation. Colin has already started college visits to many of the strongest engineering programs in the country with hopes of becoming an aeronautical engineer. In middle school, he was recognized as one of the top students, based on his character and academic performance. They are both such bright, dedicated, and loving people. Considering the turmoil Meredith and Colin had to deal with growing up, due to my health, it is a testament to what is present in their internal core! Becky and I couldn't be more proud. In fact, if I look back at our wild ride, and the enormous commitment made to my training, the quality of the person inside both of our kids is our greatest accomplishment. I never dreamed in December of 1994, I would have the chance to witness their young, blossoming lives. It has been a gift beyond words. As for my wife, I am privileged to grow old with her every day. We now have a swing to enjoy beautiful nights together and I cherish every grey hair on our heads. I don't think she feels the same…that is about the gray hair, but our relationship is beautiful and life giving. Becky and the kids are the gifts from God, which have continued to sustain me.

What will the future bring? I can only say the mountain's pitch grows steeper and the traction less certain with each and every step. When my body finally says enough, I will go home with a contented soul and will finally be ready to reunite my broken wings. I'm just not ready to quit playing the game yet!

Chapter 27

A Beautiful Life

Life is an incredibly varied journey across a complex terrain of experiences, emotions, relationships and physical challenges. It would be insincere to imply that you have total control of your own pathway, because forces along the way, some gentle and some quite violent, drive you off your intended target. Few of us are able to take a predictable path through the forest and emerge on the other side close to where we intended. It might make for less stress, but part of life's exquisite beauty is in the side roads. Some of our most treasured views come from venturing into the rugged backwoods and peering over the canyon's edge at the snow-capped mountains displaying their brilliance far off in the distance.

I had no intention of ever going to medical school. Life's experiences gave me some unique perspectives that made me feel like I needed to become a healer for my fellow man. Certainly, some very dear friends and some complete strangers, because of their willingness to reach out when I was drowning in events, inspired me and they pulled me back into the boat. I still stand in awe of the giving nature of so many. Dr. Jorge Cortes really talked me off the cliff when I was facing death from leukemia when I was ready to give up on my best options. His spirit was life giving, and a major reason I became a physician.

My wife has an indomitable, loving faith and energy, which readily spills over for everyone in her life to enjoy. I've never met anyone like her, who just made you so thankful for sharing a moment with them. That gift is the primary reason our children have grown into happy and healthy young adults. They are the beautiful reflection of her nurturing soul. Despite the major challenges we have and will continue to face, Meredith and Colin will succeed and become beacons of light for others, due to their ability to focus and adapt, during some of our darkest moments. My chest explodes with pride to know that if something happens to my physical presence in their lives, they will be fine and will find happiness on their own trails.

Do you ever find the meaning for your life? I don't think so, but it doesn't mean you should stop seeking the answers. Cylinders spin in the Himalayas, robed men spend endless hours in meditation, and monks sequester themselves on top of mountains in search of answers for that very deep question. Part of what we seek is just the simple walk and human interaction along the way. That is what makes us unique on this planet. However, I do think there are a few things that allow us to maximize our lives:

LOVE

Surround your most intimate world with family and friends you don't just care for, but you must love them deeply. Emotions can be painful at times, but it is the human experience of allowing yourself to love and be loved, which makes the highs and lows more exhilarating or bearable. It is also the foundation of Christian faith and a message given repeatedly throughout the New Testament. Even a blind woman could see things plainly:

"What we once enjoyed and deeply loved we can never lose,
for all that we love deeply becomes a part of us."

~ Helen Keller

DREAM

Our existence would be horribly mundane without the desire and ability to dream. What I found from visiting 50 countries as an Air Force pilot is that people are so similar all over the world. Their color, religion, language and culture may vary dramatically, but they share a common desire and they dream for a better life for their family and kids. That whimsical image in your mind can drive the machine inside your body to climb mountains that should be insurmountable. If a vision is present to guide the way, nothing is out of reach for the human spirit to achieve.

HOPE

At times, anger took over my life, especially when I felt my doctors had decided against offering me any future. Sometimes, they did it because they were lazy and unwilling to commit their efforts to finding better answers for me. There were also times when they just didn't know any better, but refused to send me to someone else more uniquely qualified. Taking hope away from someone is like bleeding the life out of their being. People will quickly wither when they can't find a reason to exist. Hope allowed me to chase down options, despite the monumental odds against us. It fed my mind, heart and soul so I could stand up again after falling repeatedly.

FAITH

Most of us walk through life and readily accept what we were told as children. Some will venture out and vigorously debate their most basic beliefs. Do you believe in God? Is Jesus really the Son of Man and our Savior? They are difficult questions that deserve intense contemplation. Too many people take a pedestrian path through what they believe and find at the end that they never understood the message. I can't tell someone what to believe, but I can assure you that my belief system is based on what I experienced and deeply pondered for the past 18 years. So many seemingly random events repeatedly came together to save my life. I finally opened my heart and accepted God's love. I'm still embarrassed by the unending grace He shares with me through others, but I'm working to accept my faults, as I learn more about what my faith means to me. That means more mental walks through that quiet Houston neighborhood and the sandy streets where I lost my anger and stopped questioning the torturous journey.

Would I change anything I've been through? That is a terribly difficult question. At this point, my driving desire is to make sure my family is taken care of when I leave this world. Despite my personal faith, I stay awake at night, sometimes praying for their safety and wellness so they can continue to cut their own pathway. I am who I am, based on what happened to me through 46 years of living. Cancer didn't define who I am, but it abruptly changed my course. So, I probably wouldn't change a thing, and I hope when I get a chance to discuss my life with God, He can tell me that I found my way and used in a pleasing manner the skills given me. At that point, I'll finally be able to look up from the floor, get off my knees, embrace Him, and look into His eyes and say, "Thank you for the unconditional love and your endless grace on the rollercoaster. I love you!"

Senior at Jeffersontown High School.

Me at age 6.

Mom and Dad. They have been a rock for us and sacrificed so much. We stayed with them for six months after I received chemotherapy for the tumor.

Our wedding day.
July 21, 1990

House where I grew up. My parents still live here.

Hanging out with my best girl after a trip.

My ENJPPT class at Sheppard AFB. I'm on the far left.

C-5 Galaxy. I flew these out of Dover AFB.

Becky and me with a T-38 - the most fun plane I've ever flown. Becky is pregnant with Meredith.

Oktoberfest with the Miller family. 1994

Our first house in Dover, DE. After my diagnosis, we wouldn't return there for another 10 years. Our dear friends, Barry and Jackie St. Germain, sold the house for us and saw that our belongings made it to Louisville. The wood fence to the right was built by myself, LeRoy, and Pops.

Life is good…notice the pyramids in the background. Nice.

We stayed at The Fisher House on Keesler AFB before, during, and after my first failed resection attempt. Colin was born here at Keesler.

We received presents, clothes and necessities because of many generous folks from my squadron at Dover AFB. Dec. 1994

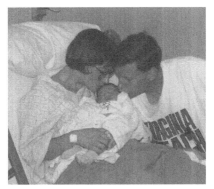

Colin's arrival on Dec 31st, 1994, helps to give us new energy and focus.

Meredith's favorite pony, Smokey. He helped us keep her busy many times while we were in Houston at MD Anderson.

Mike & Bernadette Dahlem holding Colin. They spent New Year's Eve with us at the hospital.

We lived at The Nightingale Fisher House on Wright-Patterson AFB during my chemotherapy treatments for the tumor.

Precious time with my kids while at Wright-Patterson AFB.

Retirement ceremony with Col. Steve Nelson and Barry St. Germain.

Kevin joins us for Easter egg coloring in Dayton.

Becky's dad, Ken "Pops" Schmitt

One of my presentations about making a difference.

My buddy, Mike Dahlem.

China cabinet Pops and I made together for Becky.

Continuing our tradition of having a fresh tree for Christmas.

Go Boilers!

One of my favorites things, still, is carving pumpkins with Meredith and Colin.

Surprise party held by my medical school class celebrating my 3rd year of leukemia remission.

Colin with Brian Krenzel.

Big success for the whole family... medical school graduation!

We love to watch those Boilers!

My brother and friend, Kevin.

Yellowstone National Park

Still best friends. 2011

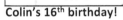

Colin's 16th birthday!

Navy ROTC Change of Command Ceremony at Purdue. Spring 2011

Family trip to Europe.

The Masters in Augusta, 2011. Colin, LeRoy, Scot Miller, Kevin, and me.

Bill & Rose Baranyk, Becky, me, Tim Porter, Steve & Elaine Melonides.   Melonides' home in Chicago, Apr. 2012

His Grace on a Rollercoaster   253

Epilogue

The story you just read, while unbelievable, is 100% true and written solely by Dr. Mark L. Jaggers. There was no ghostwriter or anyone else other than an editor at the completion of his writing.

Unfortunately, Mark isn't with us to write this epilogue, but I will use mostly his writings and that of others, to finish his story. Cancer and Death's best friend is time, it's always on their side, but I think Mark beat them to the finish line.

This is an email I received from Mark on August 17th 2010, titled "Rollercoaster...but w good news". The title of his future writing was already rolling around in his head. ("*tx*" stands for treatment):

Greetings everybody

Well I know some of you have talked, texted or rcvd emails from myself or Becky but here is the latest!

The past several weeks have been very eventful w increasing GI bleeds causing me to need blood. We are 6 wks from my previous embolization procedure. The past week got worse and caused us to push up the 2nd tx to today.

Things went very well and in Dr Coldwell's words "perfect." He was able to address the bleeding issue with twice the embolization material he used on the main tumor during the first attempt. We always have to be careful because we can walk up to the line but never step over or risk...

He was also able to continue working on the liver lesions and told me he is still just as optimistic today as he was 6 wks ago for very good things to come from this!!!!!!!!!!!!!!!! No guarantees but considering our last 16 yrs, we have a tx, a bright motivated doctor and a great option. Now we have to pray for success from

His Grace on a Rollercoaster   255

today's tx and future tx's!

In the meantime, I'm hanging out w Becky, trying to get back to work, watching Colin play HS soccer and waiting for the first opportunity to visit our Baby Boiler in W Lafayette (according to her she's having a blast...can't imagine).

Hope you are well and God Bless

Mark (Jags)

This is an email from Mark on June 22nd 2011, titled "Do You Believe in Miracles?!":

Friends

The past 17 yrs have been filled with a lot of interesting stories, people, journeys, etc. I could tell you for hours the things people have done for us as we staggered to deal with all kinds of news. I don't mind telling you that I've questioned "why?" on a number of occasions. During that period I have been told that I had a very limited amount of time left by several doctors but somebody always seemed to step up at just the right time to keep our ship afloat. MD Anderson found a way to keep me alive for 15 yrs but even they didn't have an answer when liver mets arrived 18 months ago.

I was then introduced to Dr Coldwell at UofL. He was brought here recently to get the interventional radiology program up and running using cutting edge techniques. He treated me from June to Dec of 2010 when the world was starting to unravel and I was bleeding. Well he stopped that problem, killed all the liver mets and even destroyed the center of the main mass. After all those treatments, my oncologist from UofL, wanted to try a new drug called Votrient due to some anecdotal evidence it might have activity in my sarcoma. I'm always willing to given any reasonable treatment a try. An interesting side effect, white hair!!!!!!!!!!!!

Well here we are 6 months into Votrient and 6 months after the last embolization treatment by Dr Coldwell, and I just received news I never thought I would ever hear. The mass is smaller. Huh. Yes the mass is smaller and all those liver lesions that he killed are smaller as well. We've waited 17 years to hear that news. Will it continue, who knows but yes I will keep my white hair for a while longer and get scanned in 3 months again. God truly does have a plan here I just wish I knew what it is! Well maybe not. I'm just thrilled to be here and hopefully we can share some more awesome memories/stories in the future together!

A Grateful Survivor

Mark

In January of 2012 Mark and I had some phone conversations and he told me about his plan to attempt to put down his experience on paper for the kids. We had many more conversations about events, the timeline of visits, his moments of inspiration to write, and when he was struggling with writing down different parts of the experience.

One of the conversations that I remember was, he had been having a particularly tough time getting through a certain time period to write about. He had finally sat down to work on it one morning at the office (though he had a full schedule of patients coming up that day). It was many hours later when he finally realized so much time had gone by and no one had come in to get him, he walked out of his office and asked his staff what was going on?

They told him that a series of bad t-storms and tornados had come through Louisville and that all of his appointments for the morning had cancelled due to the weather so they hadn't come to bother him. I will tell you my feelings about this after you look at his next note.

Here is an email from Mark on April 6th 2012 titled "Rough Draft for my book", which the draft attached (He said "rough draft" but it was anything but):

Barry and Jackie
Steve and Elaine
Father Dick

I have a very big favor to ask of you. I finally finished putting together the rough draft of my memoirs. It took me about two months and a lot of tears. I know all of you are very busy, but I would be grateful if you could consider reading it and giving me your thoughts. Sometimes I wonder if I rambled aimlessly and at other times didn't connect the dots for someone to follow my train of thought. I never claimed to a writer, but each of you has a unique perspective on what happened in the story written.

If you are too busy, please say so and don't worry about it. I wanted to be create an enduring gift for Meredith and Colin so they understand what happened to us. As a perfectionist, I hope the product is worth keeping around the house. If it turns out somebody can help me make more of this and have it published, I'm OK with that, but that wasn't the prime reason for writing it. The document is saved as a Word 2007 file. I can send you a different version of Word if that is helpful. Running spell and grammar check seemed to create semicolon heaven. Maybe they are correct, but I deferred to the computer when I wasn't sure. If your grammar is more correct, please let me know so I can make appropriate changes.

I had a major procedure done two days ago, and it went well. I'm very sore and expect to have another one in 4-6 weeks. Otherwise my medical problems continue to get more complicated, but I'm pushed forward by faith, love and the energy from people around me.

I find it ironic that I'm sending this to you on Good Friday and the culmination of our holiest period of the year. I've felt reborn so many times in my life and look forward to celebrating Easter this Sunday with my family.

Happy Easter and God Bless

Mark

One night shortly after I received the *rough draft* I sat down around 10pm thinking I would just read a little before I went to bed. I didn't go to bed until 2am.

When I had finished proof reading the memoirs, I remember thinking about how quickly it was written, and how perfectly it was done without any editing up to this point. I was happy and excited for him, while at the same time sad, for I immediately felt that since it was so well written, the Lord had been guiding his hand, keeping patients out of his way, and my friend had little time left with us.

Mark and Becky visited us while in Chicago for an ophthalmologist's conference on April 22nd 2012. It was shortly after he had that treatment mentioned above and had finished the draft of this memoir. When I opened the door to welcome them to our home, I could see things weren't good.

We had a *magical night* (his words) at dinner with a couple other fraternity brothers there to join us. I gave him a big hug when I left him and Becky at their hotel, and teared up all the way home, knowing I might not ever see him again.

Things continued to go poorly in the next month, kidney failure, blood transfusions, etc. At one point his kidneys started to work again but fluids were being retained and appetites were few. I said to my wife, "I don't think he's going to make it to his birthday".

The following are a series of texts I received from Mark as things started to wind down:

Mark May 23rd 2012:

Good news. My kidneys are waking up. Creatinine went 3 to 2.3 over past 10 days. Still having swelling but now likely due to albumin levels. My mouth is almost free of soreness and my protein intake is improving. Pushing scan back two wks to allow further healing and keep from pushing back into renal failure. Progress is slow but steady! Finally moving in the right direction

Mark June 13th 2012:

Just existing on the couch mostly. On experimental tx w only real hope to slow things down. Rcvd bld last wk and will get another transfusion of med and poss bld again if needed.

My response: This is not good…

Mark: *Not. These r last ditch efforts!*

On the evening of July 5th, Becky called to tell me that they, as a family, had decided to start hospice and that they were going to do so the following morning.

The choice to start hospice care was a tough one for Mark, he had always fought on, and to him, hospice was giving up but he realized the reality of things.

On the morning of Friday, July 13ᵗʰ 2012, Dr. Mark L. Jaggers passed away in his home in Louisville Kentucky. He had been struggling after that treatment earlier in the year and things just started to slowly go down hill.

Many friends and family visited during those last weeks and at the end, his wife Becky was at his side as he raised his arms in front of him as if to hug someone. She said, "Go ahead Mark, go to Jesus. Grab His hand and run!", and he passed on to our Lord shortly thereafter.

The wake and funeral were a tough time, Father Dick had a hard time keeping his composure when he spoke about Mark. Tim Porter gave a perfect eulogy as you can read in the following excerpt:

"So yes, there is certainly lots of material Jags has left us with. All of us. Each and every one of us here today has memories of Mark Jaggers that will stay with us forever. But this is where I want to make a turn and steer us all away from having today be something that is just an effort to remember Jags in our joint pasts.
What we need to do today is to realize where Jags is now, right this very second, and how hard he worked the last 17 years to give us all an example that will help us join him. So let's start by taking a brief second to really let ourselves accept, and even visualize where Jags is now. Close your eyes. Come on, close your eyes, and just picture it. What is he doing? What is he wearing? Can he hear us? And most importantly has he got a UK, a U of L or a Purdue baseball hat on? My sweet little 8 year old daughter Rose, who happens to be Mark and Becky's god-daughter, gave me a very good lesson in visualizing this picture of heaven. One day right after our dog had died we were laying down for good-night prayers, and she said "Daddy, is Trooper in heaven?" I said, "I'm sure he is". She said "You'd told me you can do anything in heaven, as long as it's not something bad. Even if you couldn't do it on Earth. Like fly, or breathe under water. I bet Trooper's doing that now. And I bet he can even talk

now, and can eat as much people food as he wants. So if he can do all these things now, why would we be sad at all?" Out of the mouth of babes.

So I'd bet you $100 that Jags has flown in a T-38 jet, played 3 rounds of golf and listened in on a U2 concert already. I'd used the word 'departure' earlier, and that was intentional. Not just for the pilot overtones it implies, but because it denotes to me the beginning of a trip. Jags and I often talked about dying just being a transition. One that is generally viewed as sad, but in reality ought to seen as be something fantastic, and that we should actually be excited about. Like finally getting to go to Hawaii. Or to Ireland or Rome. I don't really know what we'll be able to do when we get to heaven, but I do know two things. First, that it's more unbelievable than any of us can ever imagine, paling in comparison to even the most joyful moment we've ever had on Earth. And second... that Jags is there.

So now that we realize where Jags is, it's time to recognize how hard he worked for the last 17 years to give us an example that will help us join him. Mark Jaggers is probably the most singularly gifted person I've ever known. There is no doubt he is the smartest guy I know. Always getting ridiculous grades in one of the hardest majors, aeronautical engineering, at a University known for being extremely challenging. Then getting chosen for one of the most prestigious and exclusive military pilot training programs in the Air Force. Then graduating in the top of that class! Then deciding to go back to school to get a medical degree and graduating in the top of that class. And to ice it all, finding his way into one of the most sought after and exclusive branches of medical practice, ophthalmology. Moving beyond his brain, the guy also happened to be a phenomenal athlete, playing in a state championship high school basketball game and rowing on the Crew team for Purdue. Are you serious? A Big Ten athlete, a straight-A student, a jet pilot and an eye surgeon? In the words of the famous John McEnroe, "You have GOT to be kidding me!" But what God saw in Jags with all of these ridiculous abilities was wholly different from what the rest of us saw. We saw a great guy who was phenomenal at everything he did, and was a heck of a lot of fun to be around. What God saw was an instrument. A high-powered tool that had the mind, the grit and most of all, the heart to take on a burden that few could handle. And in accepting that burden, blaze a trail thru life in full view of all of us and hundreds of others, specifically to be an example. We all know the story of the burden Jags was asked to bear. And I for one know why God didn't pick me for that job because I wouldn't have been strong enough. I would have died after round one. But Jags didn't. He didn't even die after round two or three. He had a job to do. To steal a line from the Blues Brothers movie, he was on a mission from God.

Hopefully you all made it to mass yesterday, because if you did you would have heard in the Gospel a story that would have reminded you of Jags. It's the passage from Mark (Chapter 6, verse 7-13) where Jesus summoned his disciples and sent them out to do His work. He sent them with no food, no money, just a walking stick. But he also gave them his power. They did great work, but it was not for the faint of heart. They ran into plenty of troublesome places where they had to do as Jesus instructed them, dusting off their sandals, strapping them back on and moving on to the next place.

Ask yourself if you've ever known anyone who has had to dust off their sandals more times, and after bigger obstacles than Mark Jaggers. I haven't. And I doubt I ever will. If you ever find yourself asking why God made Jags go thru all that he did, stop and make yourself realize that He did it for us. And He did it because He had created in Jags one of those special humans who was able to take on this role. Not only take it on, but embrace it, and even excel at it. But then again, what else would we expect from Jags. He excelled at everything.

So we know where Jags is, now and for eternity. And we also understand why he had to walk such a thorny path in getting there. It's now our turn to put on those sandals and grab the torch Jags left us. That God himself left us. God gave us a long line of superstars. Suffering servants who had what it takes to lead those of us who are weaker of heart, so that we might turn into superstars ourselves. The most important of these was his son Jesus who suffered more than any, and paid the ultimate price. For us.

I want you all to leave here and promise to yourself and then promise to God that you will use the example Jags gave us. Use it to live your life in a way that will allow you to join Jags in heaven. And to make an example for everyone else to see, that will help them get there too. Just like Jags did. Just like Jesus did.

Jags, thank you my brother. And thank you God for being so good, and making us all the fortunate few who were blessed with Mark Jaggers. Amen."

It rained on the drive to the cemetery, but was brilliant sunshine as the USAF honor guard laid Mark to rest, paid their respects to Becky, gave him a 21-gun salute and finished with Taps.

When I said earlier, that Mark beat cancer and death to the finish line I meant this. He completed the raising of his children by showing them an incredible example. Colin is going into his senior year in high school and has always been the marker of time for this adventure. He has known and will always know his father. Meredith is going to be a junior in Nursing at Purdue and is in Navy ROTC, she knows him too. While Mark left a piece of himself with so many people, his greatest legacy is his children, he guided them and raised them well.

And Becky, well I have always had a soft spot for the caregiver. She is the definition for the vows of marriage. His struggle has been her struggle and she has been by his side every step of the way, encouraging, working and raising the family. When I first met her, way back, I was a little leary about this woman who was chasing my buddy down and trying to get her claws in him. It didn't take long for me to know what a wonderful woman she is, I/we can't thank her enough for the years of dedication to my friend, they weren't easy. I know she will find her way after the dust settles and it still won't be easy, but I know many of us will be there to help her.

I will finish with two quotes, the first is from our Fraternity Phi Delta Theta, and is said when someone passes on:

"In Heaven there is Rest"

The second is from the end of the Greek Orthodox Church's memorial service for the dead and is sung three times:

"May his memory be eternal,
May his memory be eternal,
May his memory be eternal"

Stephen J. Melonides